P9-DFX-324

1866 - 1991

125th

ANNIVERSARY

Take Charge of Your Emotional Life

Other Henry Holt books by
Robert Langs, M.D.

Decoding Your Dreams

Rating Your Psychotherapist

Take Charge of Your *Emotional Life*

Self-analysis Day by Day

Robert Langs, M.D.

Henry Holt and Company • New York

Copyright © 1991 by Robert Langs, M.D.
All rights reserved, including the right to reproduce
this book or portions thereof in any form.

Published by Henry Holt and Company, Inc.,
115 West 18th Street, New York, New York 10011.
Published in Canada by Fitzhenry & Whiteside Limited,
195 Allstate Parkway, Markham, Ontario L3R 4T8.

Langs, Robert.
Take charge of your emotional life : self-analysis day by day /
Robert Langs.—1st ed.
    p.   cm.
Includes index.
ISBN 0-8050-1278-8
1. Emotions.   2. Adjustment (Psychology)   3. Self-perception.
4. Subconsciousness.   I. Title.
BF531.L36   1991
152.4—dc20   90-27795
                                                              CIP

Henry Holt books are available at special discounts
for bulk purchases for sales promotions, premiums,
fund-raising, or educational use. Special editions
or book excerpts can also be created to specification.
For details contact:
Special Sales Director, Henry Holt and Company, Inc.,
115 West 18th Street, New York, New York 10011.

First Edition

Designed by Paula R. Szafranski

Printed in the United States of America
Recognizing the importance of preserving
the written word, Henry Holt and Company, Inc.,
by policy, prints all of its first editions
on acid-free paper. ∞

10   9   8   7   6   5   4   3   2   1

To Bernard, Billy, Charles, Jenifer, Julie, and Sandra—for taking charge; and to Channa and Amy—for being in charge

Contents

1 ⁰ Confronting the Need to Explore

LIFE IS A series of ups and downs—gratifying and wonderful moments on the one hand, and difficult and painful moments on the other. For most of us, the satisfactions seem intermittent, while the frustrations, hurts, anxieties, and concerns are with us most of the time. Tension, trauma, conflict, and stress are an inevitable part of life. Take an average day: With it comes a range of issues from stubbing your toe while getting out of bed to all manner of anxieties and conflicts—a disagreement with someone at home, a disturbing phone call, an argument at work or school, a shortage of funds, a forgotten dinner engagement, a stomachache, or having too much on your mind to be able to go to sleep.

The list is virtually endless. But these daily stresses influence our lives far more than we generally realize. Behind the scenes, they drive our behavior, alter our physical well-being, and motivate virtually every meaningful choice we make. Coping with emotional tension is one of the great challenges of life.

There are in general two basic ways by which to deal with these day-to-day stresses. The first is *the conscious system method*: confronting issues, mapping out available options, examining pros and cons, doing what we can to arrive at a quick solution. We make use of our available intelligence, ability to reason out problems, hunches and intuitions, and other resources that are directly accessible to the conscious mind. We take so much of this for granted that it is hard to imagine any other way of dealing with our emotional pressures.

There is, however, another, far more effective way to handle these issues—another system within ourselves that we can turn to for support and insight when the pot is boiling and we need answers to our emotional crises. *The unconscious system method* is an efficient way of reasoning that involves thinking carried out without awareness, ideas and solutions that are not conveyed in straightforward messages but in an encoded language. For this vast intelligence to be useful to us, we must have the means of decoding its salient messages.

The main component of this unconscious sage is *the encoded wisdom system*. This exquisite system of the mind deals with unspeakable truths but cannot tell us what it knows in the same way that a conscious thought immediately registers in awareness. The voice of this unconscious intelligence speaks to us in a beautiful, metaphoric, disguised language. Those of us who wish to live healthy and informed lives must learn how properly to access this encoded wisdom system so it can be put to effective use. Accessing this system is at the heart of truly effective self-analysis; it can bring your level of emotional coping to new heights. Integrating conscious and unconscious intelligence generates new and more effective ways of understanding and coping impossible through any other means.

ᴑᴑᴑᴑ

Whatever satisfactions we may receive from them, our relationships, surroundings, and the events of our lives are more often than not the source of emotional tension. The quality of our lives depends on how we negotiate these stresses day in and day out. Stress gives rise to emotional states, and emotional states always carry with them a significant unconscious component.

Stress-related emotionality is as commonplace as the food particles and bacteria that accumulate each day at the base of our teeth. Just as we brush our teeth and wash our bodies daily, we need a way to carry out a daily emotional cleansing. Otherwise, we become bogged down by the accumulation of tension to the point where emotional disturbance or disease intervenes. We need both prophylactic and therapeutic measures to get beneath the surface of the problem and clear it up at the source; superficial salves like taking a vacation, buying something we've denied ourselves, or consciously reassuring ourselves that everything will turn out just fine may make us feel better for the moment, but they do not alleviate the underlying sickness. Accessing unconscious wisdom is the road to healthy solutions to our everyday emotional problems as well as the repetitive plights that distress us all.

For each of us, there is a baseline of daily concerns—relationship issues, financial worries, conflicts with others—*garden-variety stress*. From time to time, an additional load of concentrated pressure—*traumatic stress*—is put upon us in the form of some acute issue whose immediate burden we must also handle: a serious illness or accident, the loss of a loved one, the discovery of betrayal or dishonesty in someone we love. Still another common form of stress is called *decision stress*—the tension we experience when faced with an important or difficult life choice. These various forms of pressure tax our inner resources and may derail our psychological and physical well-being if we lack the means to face the issues involved properly.

Stress is the external factor, and emotion is the internal factor, producing anxiety, depression, or even defensive elation. At times we experience an intensity of emotion that is different from the more casual feelings we register when we shop for clothing or buy a car. And with this intense emotion comes a whole concatenation of mental, behavioral, and physical responses that can either enhance or diminish our well-being almost immediately. The consequences can be as subtle as an unnoticed self-defeating act, a physical symptom whose emotional source is not recognized, or a blatant psychological symptom, such as an anxiety attack or episode of withdrawal—and virtually everything in between.

An informal trauma survey I conducted a few years ago revealed that a remarkably high percentage of middle-age adults had suffered two or more major physical or emotional crises in their lives; almost no one had been spared at least one significant incident—the death of a parent or sibling, a major operation, a serious illness or injury. And along with every one of these moments of external trauma, there was a significant form of inner distress and disturbance—depression, anxiety, a broad range of common and uncommon bodily ills, specific psychosomatic symptoms such as colitis or asthma. Stress extracts its price; we need to reduce its detrimental effects.

Human beings are highly adaptive and inventive creatures. Though we are by no means slaves to our stresses, we are also not as free from this bondage as we would like to believe. Our choices of adaptation are the widest in the animal kingdom, yet our fixations and tendencies toward the blind repetition of self-defeating behaviors is remarkably animal-like. The conscious system's seemingly rational choices consistently get us into these irrational situations because the conscious system *is* irrational at bottom. We choose a new lover for countless conscious reasons, only to find ourselves in a relationship more distressing than the last; we move to a new locale after pondering a string of pros and cons, and then discover that we've bought into more problems than we had left behind. On some level, we are unwittingly enslaved to our fearful inner needs, our conscious and unconscious sense of guilt. We are victims of our own rigid methods of coping with life.

We have been offered many methods for dealing with stress and its consequences. There is list making, consciousness raising, exercise, relaxation techniques, body control, meditation, biofeedback. While each of these strategies can be helpful in relieving emotional tension, none raises the issue at the root of the stress. Without getting to the source, there is no way of achieving a lasting solution; deep conflicts persist, and with them some degree of emotional compromise.

All of these approaches to emotional well-being draw on conscious thinking without the enhancement that comes from using decoded knowledge. They suffer from the limitations inherent to our conscious minds. Most of us have been disappointed by a life decision that was made after many hours of labored thought and assessment. All of us have wished we'd said this instead of that, done this instead of that—dreamed of being able to do it all over again. And most of us have been puzzled by how often we have failed to extricate ourselves from a troublesome or downright hurtful relationship, or why we take what seems like forever to do so. We blame our sense of loyalty, our ignorance, our poor defenses, our blind spots, and even our masochism; we don't realize that we must also blame evolution and the nature of the human mind for these ineptitudes.

Conscious thinking is ill equipped to cope with life's stresses. The conscious system's capacity for insight is hampered by its failure at self-reflection, its massive use of defenses that cloud its view, and its self-hurtful alliance with the *deep unconscious fear/guilt system* that drives its choices toward confusion and ineptitude. We know far more about what is best for others than we do for ourselves, but even our best insights are unwittingly prejudiced and unreliable.

Though we have cast about in every conceivable direction for help with our emotional lives—turning to friends, therapists, gurus, faith healers, religious leaders, teachers, and relatives—we have failed to look in the one direction that can help us the most: ourselves. We think that because we are in trouble and floundering, we couldn't possibly know how to solve the problems at hand. Nonetheless, we do have the answers; we just don't know that we have them. Unless we know how to get to them and unravel their secret language, we are destined to remain ignorant and go on in the same self-destructive manner.

Decoding our own encoded messages reveals the basis of an emotional problem and its solution in one fell swoop. Unconscious knowledge is at the heart of genuine self-analysis. It relies on the genius counselor deep within our own minds who knows as much as possible about our emotional plights and tells us so in disguised messages. It is as simple—and difficult—as that.

०००ঽ

Peggy* is a young woman in her early twenties; she has been dating both Dave and Marty. One evening each of them calls her and presses her to see him exclusively. That night she has a dream:

> She is in a strange house, shaped like a kidney. A man with flaming red hair is pursuing her with a knife. Another man, with a scar on his face, comes between her and her would-be attacker; the attacker pauses for a moment as if to decide whether to get into a fight. After much thought, he turns and runs away.

The next morning Peggy thinks about her dream. The two men must represent Dave and Marty, but who's who? Neither of them is redheaded, and neither has a scar. Dave is bright and sharp, a go-getter, but a bit of a hustler. He's a fast talker and a charmer, something of a turn-on. He can be impatient and sarcastic at times, but no one's perfect.

Marty, on the other hand, is a sweet guy, gentle and patient. He's bright but tends to be passive and let Peggy lead the way. At times he's boring, but he's a stable and reliable man.

Listing pros and cons, Peggy vacillates but eventually decides that she favors Dave. She knows he's seductive, but she feels he does it in a likable way; he's more exciting to be with and more stimulating in bed than Marty. She's convinced they could make a go of it, despite the obvious risks.

---

*The incidents and people in the anecdotes presented in this book are real, but names and identifying features have been disguised. I am indebted to those who shared these moments with me; they are the inspiration for these writings.

0000

This is the substance of Peggy's conscious system assessment of the two men. But does her encoded wisdom system have a different opinion? To find the answer, Peggy must associate to her dream. The redheaded man reminds her of a movie she had seen in which a redheaded bank president turned out to be a homicidal madman. He would seduce a woman and then murder her, always at the moment when he found a new lover. But Dave is in investment banking; does that mean that he is the knifer in the dream? Consciously, Peggy is reluctant to believe her own associations—her unconscious and encoded perceptions, if you will, of Dave.

At first Peggy can think of nothing associated with a facial scar. But eventually she remembers a story Marty had told her of an accident he had seen in the park when a woman pedestrian was inadvertently run into by a biker. Her face had been cut badly, and though Marty gave her first aid that staunched the bleeding, he was certain she would be left with a noticeable scar.

Marty helps a woman run into by a man on a bike. Dave is an ardent biker. It's becoming clear to Peggy that her unconscious view of her two boyfriends is the very opposite of her conscious assessment. Yet it now occurs to her that Dave, who had denied seeing other women, had been out several nights when he had expected her to call him. Peggy had dismissed as ridiculous her passing thoughts that maybe he was actually out with another woman; this worry comes back to her only now. She had always spoken of deception as a slap in the face. Had she unconsciously perceived Dave's infidelity, even as her conscious mind was assuring her that everything was just fine? Within the week, a friend tells Peggy of seeing Dave at dinner with a very attractive woman.

Consciously, Peggy was blind to the clues that Dave was two-timing her, because she wanted to be unaware; awareness is painful, and we often opt for immediate pain reduction. More often than not, however, this kind of inattention leads us into trouble—and keeps us there; we end up having more pain than we might have experienced had we dealt with the issue head-on. But doing that requires overcoming the natural tendencies of the conscious mind to avoid a truth it does not want to face.

There are two fundamental reasons for engaging in self-analysis: first, because the conscious mind cannot deal effectively with our daily and extended emotional issues, and second, because these issues are with us day after day calling for resolution and change. With this in mind, we can survey some of the specific reasons for carrying out decoding self-exploration.

Perhaps the most fundamental and compelling of these reasons arises from the daily accumulation of emotional detritus that weighs us down emotionally and drains our psychological strength. Through stress and strain, we all take on a measure of emotional baggage each day of our lives. Neglected, this emotional load can turn into unexplained episodes of anxiety or depression, inexplicable tendencies toward emotional symptoms of self-defeating actions, emotional paralysis.

The most basic function of self-analysis is to keep our emotional concerns from derailing us. Small emotional issues, and their direct and unconscious ramifications, have a way of adding up to major emotional difficulties. A daily bit of self-exploration—perhaps in the quiet minutes before falling asleep—can take us a long way toward maintaining a fairly stable and symptom-free state. The effort can bring insights and perspectives into the unconscious forces that are disturbing our emotional equilibrium and threatening even greater disaster; coming to terms bit by bit with these unseen dangers is vital to emotional balance.

Each of us must deal with some degree of physical and emotional trauma every day of our lives, and on occasion with a significant catastrophe. It takes only a small amount of stress to produce any number of disturbances: anxiety, depression, phobias and obsessions, hurtful actions, physical ills of all kinds. The more adept we are at coping, the less we suffer. Learning to carry out trigger decoding can lessen our emotional pain and related physical illnesses, and reduce the possibility of irrational action.

At all decisive junctures in our lives, there are both rational and irrational elements to the choices we make. Most often the unseen unconscious forces are secretly running the show, even as we believe we are being rational and deliberate, with a clear (conscious) idea of what we want. But the more we know of the unconscious side, the more we bring our unconscious wisdom into conscious awareness through effective decoding, the broader our sense of the situation will be—and the more likely our choice will be wise, satisfying, and enduring. Without deep self-analysis, we are all slaves to our conscious defenses and deep unconscious anxieties; yet with self-analysis, we can take over as genuine masters of our own life decisions.

The failure to develop the methods of effective self-analysis is not merely a matter of ignorance or laziness. There exists within each of us strong opposition—resistances—to engaging in any process that can lead to the direct awareness of encoded unconscious knowledge. We have repressed these perceptions of ourselves and others because of the pain they would cause were we aware of them; yet this unconsciously registered comprehension empowers our emotional life far more than conscious thought. The battle is joined: dread of encoded meaning on one side, the need to know on the other. In general, it takes a lot of effort to win this battle because our basic fear of this knowledge— the murderous, incestuous, deceiving, and terrible side of ourselves and others—far outweighs our belief that facing these truths can lead to effective mastery.

This antagonism extends to the very process of self-exploration. We decide to remember our dreams, but fail to do so; we remember a dream, but forget to associate to it and subject it to little more than the most cursory exploration; we suffer from a depression or act in a way that is evidently irrational and self-defeating, but we either fail to notice the problem or deny we've had anything to do with its outcome—we see ourselves as victims of fate. Our habitual ways of defending ourselves come into play, and conscious vigilance and self-awareness are needed to recognize their manifestations. We can consciously oppose our own resistances and insist through sheer effort on engaging in self-analysis and trigger decoding. And the more we learn about our own rationalizations and reluctance to know, the better our chances of overcoming these oppositional forces.

Here again we find ourselves with minds in conflict. On the one side is the press for quick relief, regardless of the price; on the other is the patient search for deep understanding and sensitively reasoned solutions. There is no avoiding the consequences of the path we choose, though we may try to deny the more terrible effects by exploiting our conscious system's defenses. Yet perseverance is also possible, and with it the possibility of understanding the unconscious basis of our fears of emotional truth—whether they are truths about ourselves or about others who are important in our lives. Truth in hand, we can solve most of the emotional mysteries with which we are faced. And the practical results are impressive: a chance to find new ways of coping, of taking life more in stride, of being able to endure the worst of it and recover, and of keeping the lapses to a minimum—a way of achieving a kind of calm and understanding few of us are privileged to possess otherwise.

2 ∘ The Dual System of the Mind

OF THE TWO basic reasons for doing self-analysis, by far the easier to recognize is the daily emotional concerns that serve as a call to self-exploration. Far less appreciated is the more fundamental need for decoding analysis created by the limitations and deceits of conscious system coping. This necessity arises not only by virtue of the psychic defenses used by the conscious system—for example, avoidance, denial, blaming others—but also as a consequence of the very structure of the human mind. Being restricted and misguided in our available options for direct emotional adaptation is in our basic nature—it is how the mind is built.

The human mind appears to be one of the great unfinished jobs of human evolution. It is structured as two systems, one with awareness, the other without it. The *conscious system* is designed to deal with immediate reality, though it has some capacity for memory and anticipation. The system is a remnant from our heritage as hunters and gatherers, and is designed basically to insure survival—to carry out effective emergency reactions to danger and to secure skills that enable us to find safety, food, shelter, companionship, and other practical necessities and satisfactions. This intense alertness to external reality and to issues of endurance is achieved at the expense of our capacity to deal with emotions. The conscious mind cannot operate efficiently if it is distracted by the feeling side of life.

Evolution has not entirely neglected this compelling part of life in its provisions for psychic coping. As the conscious mind must be clear and trouble-free so it can handle its practical tasks, emotions are managed mainly outside of awareness—in the unconscious part of the mind—by *the deep unconscious system.* The raw perceptions of emotional assault by ourselves and others registered and worked over in this part of the mind would greatly disturb our immediate functioning. Therefore the conscious mind can prevent unconscious information from coming through directly into awareness. As a result, communication between the two systems of the mind, conscious and unconscious, takes place through disguised or encoded messages; a compromise is wrought and unconscious information comes to the surface in altered form.

Decoding unconscious messages is far more than a fascinating exercise. Two compelling reasons that arise from the structure of the human mind render self-analysis a necessity: first, our emotional lives are literally run by our unconscious needs and fears; the conscious mind serves mainly to rationalize and excuse behaviors that we are compelled to carry out by virtue of unrecognized unconscious reasons. Emotional symptoms, such as anxiety, phobias, and depression, are also founded on these same unconscious constellations. A life lived without decoding and deep self-analysis is a life enslaved to unrecognized and unmastered unconscious forces. A full life requires access to the needs and secrets of the unconscious mind, brought into the beacon light of direct awareness where they can be used to influence the course of our lives favorably. Left in the dark, these needs can only cause pain.

The second reason that self-analysis is essential to our well-being is that virtually all of the answers to our emotional dilemmas are encoded in the depths of our own unconscious minds. Self-analysis through trigger decoding shows us the best possible solutions to our emotional ills. Within the unconscious mind lies both the terrible roots of our emotional woes and yet the wondrous means, however encoded, of resolving them.

This dual system has arisen because of the way the human mind is configured. There are two fundamental splits in the structure of our minds: The first divides the conscious part of the mind from the unconscious part. The second occurs entirely within the unconscious system, with an *encoded wisdom system* on the one hand and a *fear/guilt system* on the other. The wisdom system is deeply perceptive and knowledgeable, reliable in its views and recommendations, and our greatest untapped human resource. The fear/guilt system is the seat of our most terrifying nightmares. Embodied in this system are the residuals of every dreadful experience in our lives, every moment of hurt to and from others, every failure to adhere to rules and laws, and every sense we have of our own limitations, vulnerabilities, and mortality.

As sources of needs and motives, each of these systems leads us in opposite directions—one toward health and wise choices, the other toward illness and hurtful decisions. Where one seeks to guide us toward forgiveness and growth, the other presses us toward self-punishment and regression. And where one has our very best interests at heart and opts only for the gratification of healthy needs, the other will have us sabotage ourselves and ply ourselves with costly, ill-gotten satisfactions.

But when it comes to our feelings and actions, the systems are not equally matched. The conscious system—how we think and behave—is almost entirely under the influence of the unconscious fear/guilt system. This arrangement accounts in large part for the poor and hurtful qualities of many of our conscious choices and for much of our emotional grief. Pressured by guilt and anxiety stemming from unconsciously registered hurts we have caused others and by a need to suffer motivated by guilt borrowed from others for their "crimes," we unwittingly select the less satisfactory of two educational opportunities, two lovers, or two careers. For much the same reasons, we somehow find ourselves failing in a job that should be bringing us much success, messing up a relationship that was going along beautifully, or under attack for reasons we can't fathom.

This design of nature also means that without decoding, encoded wisdom barely influences our conscious choices. Occasionally some valuable hunch or intuition emerges from its confines, though these insights and feelings are rarely fully formed; to be able to act in keeping with them we have to understand the circumstances to which they refer—to use trigger decoding. Failing that, the shrewdness of the system goes to waste; avoiding such a tragic loss is a major reason for self-analysis. But beyond that, self-exploration is the only reliable means we have to combat the unholy alliance between the unconscious fear/guilt system and the conscious system—and its dire consequences. If we leave nature untouched in the emotional sphere, we leave ourselves at the mercy of an alignment set against our own best interests. Wondrously, though, the human mind can become aware of its own flaws and learn how they can be rectified; through self-analysis the situation can be favorably reordered.

Lois is a married woman in her late forties who is trying to decide whether to have a third child. Both of her daughters are now in college, and Lois has gone back to work as an advertising account executive, though with little feeling of accomplishment or satisfaction. Jeff, her husband, has left the impregnation decision to her, and she vacillates between pros and cons—the child would be wonderful to have, but a burden; she loved being a mother, but treasures her current freedom; she had easy pregnancies and healthy children, but a pregnancy at her age is risky; she had always wanted to have three children, but why risk it now; it would strengthen her marriage, but might create unnecessary problems.

Lois grows impatient with her inability to decide. One night she grits her teeth, again adds up the fors and againsts, and decides to go ahead and try to conceive. She plies herself with congratulations in having made her choice and is soon occupied only with the positive side of the situation.

That night Lois, who writes for a hobby, composes a short story. It's about a married woman, Marie, who is attracted to her internist, Matt. She struggles against his attempts to seduce her but gives in at a weak moment. Marie becomes depressed when she discovers that her closest friend, Melanie, has also had an affair with the same physician. Together they plot revenge by arranging for Marie to discover Melanie in a motel room with the busy

lover. The story ends on a wild note of confusion and triumph—of sorts.

Lois treats her story like a dream and associates freely
to its elements. Marie is the name of a woman in her husband's office who actually became pregnant at the age of
forty-nine. Jeff had been extremely critical of Marie for
getting pregnant—a reaction Lois had forgotten until now;
the child was born with Down's syndrome. Lois's mother's
name is Mary; it suddenly occurs to Lois that her mother
had nearly died giving birth to her brother—her third child.

Matt and the affair recall the painful recollection that
some months ago when Lois first returned to work, she
struggled against and then allowed herself to have a brief
affair with Andrew, the director of marketing at her firm.
Andrew is a playwright and actor who has played the part
of a doctor; the connection to the story is unmistakable.
Lois had thought that she had repented for her affair and
had quietly tried to be a better wife to Jeff. As a final
thought, Lois remembers a conversation many years earlier
with her aunt Molly, in which her aunt had described a
terrible experience with a miscarriage of a late pregnancy;
she had warned Lois that late pregnancies are a subtle way
of attempting suicide.

Analyzing and integrating this story-associational network,
it would appear that Lois's decision to go ahead and try to
conceive was unconsciously based on unresolved guilt over
her affair with Andrew—guilt her conscious system had
strongly denied. The association to her mother indicates
Lois's unconscious wish to die as punishment for her trans-
gression, while the association to Marie speaks for another
kind of punishment in having a damaged child. The images
related to her husband indicate that getting pregnant could

jeopardize Lois's marriage—still another punishment for her affair.

These are stories and associations, encoded symbols that contain Lois's unconscious perceptions of her decision and the unconscious factors that led to her choice. Where the conscious mind reveled in the glory of trying to conceive, the deep encoded wisdom system was aware that the choice was being driven by the unconscious fear/guilt system and its relentless search for punishment for transgressions. The conscious system, operating under this influence, unwittingly created a denial-filled scenario through which Lois could convince herself that seeking a pregnancy was the wisest choice—a viewpoint that managed to overlook much available knowledge and many vital clues to the contrary. Self-analysis was Lois's only hope for escaping from the trap she had consciously set for herself; only the encoded wisdom system, operating without defensiveness or guile, knew the best means to avoid making a hurtful mistake. The wise answer evidently lay encoded in Lois's recall of her conversation with her aunt Molly—don't risk a late pregnancy, it could kill you.

These associations, decoded in light of the trigger of Lois's decision for impregnation, reveal an unconscious appraisal that the risks far outweigh the advantages in this choice; and, of course, this assessment is exactly the opposite of Lois's conscious evaluation. Life with self-analysis is far different from life without it. Decode and choose wisely; react on the basis of direct thinking and you will probably suffer needlessly.

Once she had digested the decoded messages from her unconscious wisdom system, Lois changed her mind about trying to conceive. With that decision in place, she unexpectedly thought of a friend named Matthew—a name she associated to Matt, the intern. Matthew had developed leukemia and was concerned about dying. He had joked recently about having a child to replace the vacancy he would soon create. Lois has asthma and it had been acting up lately; on this level, her wish to become pregnant seems to be serving as a defense against death anxieties and as a magical form of reparation of the kind fantasied by Matthew. The fear aspect of her unconscious mind had also influenced Lois's decision—fears that were hinted at in her recall of the near-death pregnancy experiences of both her mother and aunt. These deep fears of mortality, of fallibility, silently drive many conscious choices and account in part for virtually all emotional symptoms and difficulties.

The conscious system is with us from birth, growing, learning, developing an intelligence and ways of coping that are reinforced by our immediate experiences with reality. The system finds support from our parents and unconsciously models its modes of adaptation on the ways our mentors deal with the real and emotional worlds. But always the conscious mind is part of a system that prefers false reassurances and covert forms of self-punishment to an honest assessment of an emotional situation.

Once we develop a capacity for unconscious perception and symbol formation, at about two or three years of age, the connections between the developing unconscious fear/guilt system and the conscious mind are solidified. Into this fear-dominated system goes every unconscious perception that is unbearable to awareness—moments of violence, crass sexuality, illness, parental abuse, and other types of deep hurts. Much the same occurs with the guilt we experience for our own hurtful behaviors and wishes, and for the "sins" of our parents as well. All of our transgressions, our violations of laws and boundaries and spaces, evoke guilt that is stored in this unconscious system, leading it to search relentlessly for opportunities to evoke punishment. And to this awful mix are added the realizations of the inevitability of our own death and the extent of our physical and emotional vulnerabilities. All told, the fear/guilt system is a powerhouse of ill will, a place from which emotional derailment arises. And almost always, we act or suffer without knowing the deeper reasons; the conscious system is the great denier, rationalizer, and excuse maker, the unwitting architect of our own emotional pain.

In the meantime, the encoded unconscious wisdom system is also developing its capacities and skills. Subliminal or unconscious perception is its mode of experiencing, and the system operates without the defensive screening and denial needed by the conscious mind. And these undistorted and incisive perceptions provide us with a sound picture of what is healthy and growth promoting, enhancing and in our best interests; they also tell us what is truly harmful, when boundaries are inappropriately violated, and when self-harm and fear take over. Though delivered in disguise, deep wisdom can be trusted.

Having defined the systems of the mind and their role in sickness and health, we need to make some final preparations before plunging into the work of self-analysis. We want to afford the conscious system an opportunity to surrender or modify some erroneous basic assumptions that tend to undermine effective self-exploration.

First off, there is the false idea that we really want to know the truth about ourselves and others as fully and honestly as possible. Actually, deep within ourselves we all dread unconscious meaning. We do everything possible to

avoid knowing that we will eventually die and other dis-
comforting realizations that would cause us pain and panic.
The contents of the unconscious domain are placed there
precisely because they are intolerable. Were these most telling perceptions and insights tolerable, we would not have
relegated them to this elusive part of the mind.

Who among us wants to know that someone we dearly
love wants to murder us or devour our innards, that one
or both of our parents are using us for sick kinds of grat-
ifications, that our boss is so furious over the mistake we
made that he wants to plant a bomb under our seat—or
that we in our fury at him want to dismember him? The
world of unconscious experience is primitive and horrify-
ing, blunt in its appraisals and raw in its reactions. While
such images would overwhelm our conscious functioning
were they in awareness, suppressing them leads us into
emotional symptoms, costly defensive postures, and unconsciously driven acts of revenge or self-harm for which we
pay dearly.

We dread unconscious truths and fear being overwhelmed by their implications, so we forgo the great
knowledge of the encoded wisdom system in favor of suppressing the clues to better living that it emits. Set in its
ways of aversion, the conscious system will offer any number of rationalizations to justify avoiding sound self-
processing. It will argue that we're just fine, we don't need
help from below; we've thought things through a thousand
times and know everything there is to know. We learn not
to trust our own thoughts.

Despite direct claims to the contrary, the conscious system raises a tireless voice of opposition to the search for
deep truths. Propelled by the unconscious fear/guilt system
on one side, and by a dread of unconscious experience on

the other, the conscious system uses all its wiles to prevent us from getting to unconscious meaning. Though the conscious system seldom cries out for help, knowing when we are deceiving and defeating ourselves is the first step toward cure.

Under the sway of the conscious system, we tend to opt for blind and quick relief, but we pay a price in the form of persistent, seemingly sourceless aggravation and tension. This balance between compensation and cost is called *the help/hurt ratio*. Every effort we make to relieve ourselves of emotional suffering—whether through blind action or deep insight—has some cost factor attached to it. As a rule, following the insights of the encoded wisdom system has the best possible help/hurt ratio, while conscious system cures rate poorly. The goal of self-analysis is to maximize the help and minimize the hurt.

The conscious system often makes bad bargains in which the help/hurt ratio is low—the real hurt, recognized or ignored, is greater than the actual help. The system is vulnerable to making such choices largely because it defensively tends to ignore the price side of the ratio. A woman cheats on her fiancé and feels excited that she is attractive to her new lover, but she fails to notice that she then repeatedly provokes her fiancé into condemning and attacking her. A father repeatedly loses control and beats his children, but never realizes that the psychosomatic diarrhea his doctor cannot alleviate is in part an inner punishment for his hostility.

It is inevitable that misconceptions about our daily emotional lives and their management exist. Emotions generally blunt our conscious intelligence, interfere with our best adaptive resources, and badly color our judgment. When we are under stress, deep and powerful *unconscious* forces are unleashed, most of them stemming from the unconscious fear/guilt system that interferes with sound coping.

We like to think of ourselves as open to the truth and as relatively nondefensive. But by and large, the conscious system is a denial system. It denies the cost of its defenses and its hurtful actions, the extent to which life brings stress, and the very need for self-analysis. Some people have the opposite mistaken belief: For them, life is hopelessly hurtful and there is no way to ease the unbearable pain. Yet except in extreme cases, neither of these notions—that there is no meaningful stress and that overwhelming and unsolvable stress exists—is true. For most of us, normal stress is ever-present but manageable, while the dramatic moments of traumatic or crisis stress will pass in time and can be transformed into interludes of growth through effective self-exploration.

Whether we acknowledge it or not, most of us believe that what we see and experience and know directly accounts for all that is important in life. We rely on our sense impressions and make no effort to probe deeper. We think that our conscious decisions will control and direct the future of our emotional lives. This is the conscious system's way of trying to shut out the unconscious domain and establish itself as fully responsible for emotional issues. The system is willing to court blame in exchange for its claim of power over our lives—a claim that flies in the face of the truth.

This mistaken set of beliefs involves a fundamental denial of unconscious mental processes and forces. The universal denial takes many forms: Only conscious thinking really exists, unconscious thinking (information processing) is a Freudian myth; all communication is manifest and direct, the rest is in our imagination; unconscious messages and communication simply can't be proven to be there, so why bother with them; even if there are nonconscious messages and thinking, they're not especially important and we needn't busy ourselves to get in touch with what they have to say—to cite a few of the most frequent ways this kind of denial surfaces. Yet no matter how strongly the conscious system may deny unconscious forces, they make their presence known in our emotional misery. Either we bring them to the surface and deal with them, or they stay submerged and deal with us.

Still another myth claims that the systems of the mind, including the conscious and encoded wisdom systems, work in harmony and support each other's functioning. But, actually, disharmony and discord prevail between these two critical structures. Conscious needs, wishes, and intelligence are diametrically opposed to those of the deep unconscious wisdom system. This is why our emotional reactions and choices differ dramatically depending on whether they are informed by conscious or encoded intelligence. The conscious system has created the myth of mental harmony to lull us away from allegiance to unconscious wisdom; only by dispelling the myth can we realize that we are dealing with two enemy camps—and each person must choose one or the other side.

We come now to a final myth we must disassemble to clear the path to decoding self-analysis. There are three aspects to this myth: First, that we need to be in, or to have had, therapy to get in touch with our own unconscious encoded wisdom. Second, that when the going gets rough, when our coping capacities are too weak to deal with the emotional issues at hand and emotional symptoms appear, we must go immediately to a psychotherapist to work things out. And third, that while we may resolve some inner emotional tensions or illuminate an emotional decision through self-analysis, there is nothing we can do to change reality—we are helpless in the face of trauma.

In fact, with few exceptions, the last place that people are likely to discover deep encoded truths is in the office of today's psychotherapists. You, as a nonprofessional, can learn the necessary techniques for decoding that professionals are not yet using. At best, what you'll get from a therapist is largely conscious system relief. I am not arguing against seeking professional help when all else fails, but I am arguing for your trying to use your own profound resources first.

Both consciously and unconsciously, you, more than anyone else, know your darkest secrets. You alone are the first therapist you should call on. Humankind has greatly underestimated the natural healing resources housed within each of us. Decoding your own unconscious messages can do many things for you. Your deep unconscious wisdom system knows everything in the emotional arena that it is possible to know. It knows when your lover is thinking of leaving you or when he or she has been unfaithful; it knows which is the best of several jobs you are considering, or when you should leave a relationship that is more hurtful than satisfying; and it knows when someone can be trusted. It even knows the unconscious structure or underlying basis of an emotional symptom—anxiety, depression, obsessions, compulsions, phobia, interpersonal difficulties.

You needn't wait for a crisis to occur in order to do better for and with yourself: The deep unconscious wisdom system works over the most seemingly trivial stress, the most minor problem or choice, much the same as it deals with more significant issues. You can use its resources on a daily basis, all to your personal advantage. Only when you find yourself blocked, your symptoms too severe, or when the problem at hand does not seem to lessen despite a reasonably extended effort at self-analysis should you seek the help of a therapist—and preferably one who understands the mechanisms of unconscious communication.

Part of the problem lies in a fundamental misconception about the nature of psychotherapy. Conventional wisdom has it that "The man who is his own doctor has a fool for a patient." This is certainly true regarding many services offered by physicians and healers—surgery, medical care for major illnesses, setting broken bones. But some aspects of health care allow for self-diagnosis and self-care. This is the case with many hygienic measures, such as hair and skin care, and with problems of exercise and nutrition. The emphasis is not on curing an illness but on instituting a program of health and optimal functioning.

The case is much the same with psychotherapy or self-analysis. By alternating between the roles of "patient" and "therapist," you can gain genuinely new insights that can help you to better resolve your emotional issues. Being therapist to yourself, using decoding effectively as the main tool, can be a very satisfying experience. Longstanding emotional problems will usually give ground to sustained self-exploration; there's no limit to how much can be accomplished if we try.

Some people feel that there is very little we can do to influence the realities with which we are confronted in daily life. Certainly, there are many traumas—an unavoidable accident, the actions of others, the inevitability of aging and death—that are not self-orchestrated. But a surprisingly large number of hurts and stresses are problems we unconsciously create for ourselves even as we blame others or rotten luck. This is true of many forms of physical illness, of a fair number of accidents, and of many destructive relationships and situations in which we find ourselves. Unconscious guilt is a powerful inner force, and it arranges many punitive incidents for us. Through proper self-analysis, we can identify these self-defeating tendencies, understand their motivation, and reduce their power over our lives.

In both small and large ways, immediately and over the long term, self-exploration can change our lives for the better. By opening up the conscious system to encoded wisdom and expanding our view of ourselves, others, and the world, we gain much in the way of better relationships and living. Now it's time to get to the nitty-gritty of this wonderful, awesome process and all it can give to us.

3 · The Driving Force for Self-analysis

Everybody has his own delusion assigned to him; but we do not see that part of the bag which hangs on our {own} back.
—Catallus, circa 56 B.C.

I HAVE A friend, Eddie, a man in his early fifties; we play tennis together from time to time. At the end of a game one day, he said, "Well, I'm free again; no more Jan. Time to call up the old girlfriends, I guess."

Free again? Eddie had been married and divorced, lived with someone for a while, married again, then lived with someone else while separated, moved back with his wife, divorced her, and finally moved in with Jan. It was easier to keep track of tennis scores.

Jan seemed to be a rather nice woman, and affectionate with Eddie. I assumed they'd eventually marry. But Eddie said, "I suppose one of the advantages of a history like mine is the fact that it gets easier to see when it's not working. You don't need to bang your head against a wall; you just end it and find someone else who really wants to work things out with you. She may have been the one to walk, but I'm sure not going to let her back in."

"I'm sorry," I volunteered. "I thought you and Jan had something going."

"Yeah, well, Jan has a good social personality; we were good at parties and here at the courts, but at home it was really unbearable. She was on me about everything. I mean, yeah, I've got a bit of a temper, but she really pushed me over the edge, you know? It's like she was *trying* to get me to slap her around a little; she wouldn't let up till I did it. You're an analyst, you know the type, right? Always nagging me about this and that; always after me for sex just when I'm tired and ready to collapse, then making cracks about me not being man enough to do it and stuff like that. Who needs it? You hook up with a woman who seems okay, and she right away wants to change you. Who wants a relationship where you can't be yourself, right? I thought Jan was different, but I'm thinking now that maybe all women are pretty much the same—trouble—and it's not worth the effort. It's making me crazy. I've had nothing but heartburn all week.

"A lot of guys at this club won't face the problems in their marriages and relationships," Eddie continued breathlessly. "They make up one excuse after the other— it's not how it looks; things will get better; there's really nothing better around; things like that. But that's not the way I am: I face a problem when it's there and do something constructive about it, no matter how much it hurts. You've got to tear down the old to make way for the new."

There's little point in going on, even though that's just what Eddie did. Packed into this little vignette is much that is amiss in all of us when it comes to recognizing an emotional problem. Obliterating a call for self-analysis is a way of blocking the path to deeper self-understanding before we can enter its convoluted byways; it is a means of destroying the immediate motivation for doing self-analysis.

Indicators are the troublesome behaviors, predicaments, choices, feelings, and symptoms that summon us to self-analytic activities; they tell us that we are in emotional difficulty or that we are facing a painful or complex life decision and that we need a comprehensive solution. Indicators are anything that cause anxiety, but specifically they include

1. Psychological/emotional symptoms. These are the inner mental or internal signs of emotional difficulty. Most of these symptoms are well known; they include disturbances of feeling/mood states such as undue anxiety, depression, unnatural fears as well as the more elaborate psychological/emotional syndromes such as phobias, obsessions, withdrawal, and the like. Also included here are disturbing inner fantasies of violence and sexuality, other strange mental preoccupations, and problems with self-esteem, self-image, and identity.

2. Self-harmful behaviors. These are the familiar addictions to cigarettes, drugs, and alcohol, and eating disorders, suicidal tendencies, and other self-inflicted harm.

3. Interpersonal difficulties. This category of indicators embraces a wide variety of disturbances in our relationships with others; it is a group of difficulties that lends itself readily to denial—much as we saw with Eddie, who ignored his role in his repeated problems with women. In general, included here is any emotionally disturbing life experience in which our own actions are open to question—an unnecessary tiff with the boss at work, an uncalled-for incident with our spouse or lover, a moment of self-orchestrated frustration or hurt, and so on. Other indicators in this category are moments of irrational or impulsive behavior; antisocial behaviors such as dishonest acts, exploiting others, and disregarding their needs or feelings; unnecessarily hurtful or seductive actions toward others; and being involved in hurtful relationships of any kind.

4. Anxiety-provoking decisions. A special category of indicators involve emotionally charged and important life decisions that disturb our equilibrium. While not exactly symptomatic, these decisions are sufficiently troublesome to warrant self-analysis not only for our inner peace but also for the light that encoded wisdom can shed on them.

5. Character disorders/personality disturbances. These are problems in the very fiber of our being, functioning, and relating that are so enduring and so integral to our personality that they often seem natural and nonpathological. Chronic suspiciousness, querulousness, incessant seductiveness, natural tendencies toward provocation, and extremes of guardedness are some types of personality disorders commonly seen today. We can best identify these difficulties by asking how others see us and assessing complaints about our personality made by different people who know us; we should assume they're right and that we have a problem until proven otherwise—or changed through self-analysis.

6. Psychotic syndromes. These disorders involve a break with reality and involve inner convictions about incidents and experiences that go far beyond real possibility. They include hallucinations, delusions, paranoid ideation, extremes of depression and withdrawal, and similar difficulties. Typically, persons suffering from such disorders have little insight into their dysfunctions and rarely become motivated to carry out self-analysis. These are serious emotional symptoms. While self-analysis may help to diminish their intensity, they often call for professional intervention.

7. *Physical illness.* Most forms of physical illness have an unconscious mental component. Illnesses ranging from dermatological disorders, to the common cold and sore throats, to gall bladder attacks and the so-called psychosomatic syndromes such as asthma, peptic ulcer, and colitis are likely to be open to some degree of modification through self-analysis; this is especially true of repetitive illnesses and those needing multiple surgical procedures as well as most types of menstrual difficulties. In principle, we should recognize that these physical ills are likely to be expressions of unconscious conflict. Their presence indicates the need for self-analytic work designed to reach their unconscious underpinnings.

Indicators are signs of emotional dysfunction, and all such disturbances are unconsciously driven in large measure. They are active and current emotional concerns and a living target for unconscious understanding. In explaining the unconscious basis for an active indicator, self-analysis has a pragmatic purpose—the cure of immediate ills. And as contemporary difficulties extend into and link up with past ills, these issues also become targets for active self-exploration.

Indicators are evoked by triggers; our emotional problems are activated by emotionally charged experiences that overwhelm our coping capacities and lead to dysfunction. Therefore, to discover the unconscious meaning of an indicator, we must uncover its trigger and ascertain what unconscious impact the trigger situation had on our psyche. Indicators are illuminated through trigger decoding— deciphering the meanings of dreams and behaviors in light of the triggers that evoked the emotional disturbance or choice.

Eric is depressed and has impulsively quit his job—these are his indicators. Exploration brings forth a dream of a man buying an expensive car. Associations are to an opulent man who owned three Rolls-Royces and to another man who robbed a car dealership and was caught and sent to jail. Eventually, Eric thinks about his father, a bank executive who has been accused of misconduct and is awaiting trial (the trigger).

Analysis of this material indicates that Eric's depression and impulsive act were unconsciously based on a perception of his father as extravagant and criminal in light of the charges against him. Eric was depressed because he viewed his father as a criminal and was punishing himself as a stand-in for his father.

Because indicators motivate the initiation of self-analysis, acknowledging their existence is the first step in the self-exploratory process. Not surprisingly, our first resistances are directed against such acknowledgments. As a result, we must deal with these obstacles even before we begin our self-investigation. Self-analysis often begins by struggling to discover why we are trying to deny that we need to carry it out in the first place.

Two additional driving forces make self-analysis a necessity. The first are emotionally charged trigger experiences. These incidents disturb our emotional equilibrium and activate our mental coping capacities; we develop emotional symptoms—indicators—when our ability to adapt to these trigger situations is overtaxed. Indicators are the immediate cause for self-analysis. But triggers are the ultimate cause in that they create the indicators from which we suffer and are at the root of our unconscious reactions. For example, Eddie's heartburn was one of his indicators, while Jan's walking out on him was the trigger. Just as indicators come in many forms, the emotionally upsetting events that activate our mental responses are also varied—they range from physical harm to the smallest personal frustration or slight. Anything that disturbs our emotional equilibrium functions as an evocative trigger experience. It is an ultimate call for the self-analytic process as a way of helping us handle these dysphoric incidents better.

A second driving force for self-analysis involves the process itself. Seldom does this work proceed smoothly and without obstacles. But the disruptions are themselves cause for self-analysis; they are best resolved with the help of the encoded wisdom system that enables us to understand their unconscious basis—the hidden roots of resistance to self-analysis.

Eddie's blaming Jan for their breakup rather than acknowledging his own responsibilities for the incident is a case in point: By denying his interpersonal indicator—his problems in relating to women—Eddie fails to acknowledge a need for self-analysis and has no reason to initiate self-exploration. Resistances may crop up in any phase of self-analysis, from failing to remember a dream, to blocking on associating, to missing the key triggers; they are infinite in variety and commonplace.

There are, then, two basic classes of indicators: symptomatic indicators and resistance indicators. The first group summons us to self-exploration, while the second group calls for restoring the self-analytic process to its proper course. Any sign of emotional tension and anything we say or do to discourage self-exploration from its start to its finish are indicators telling us that we have self-exploratory work to do.

Let's concentrate now on symptomatic indicators and how we are likely to deal with them when we contemplate self-analysis. There are, of course, emotional difficulties that we can't dismiss outright, problems that won't submit to denial and decisions whose impacts on our lives we can't possibly overlook. But given the state of our conscious minds, there are countless emotionally charged disturbances, behaviors, and choices, and many internal emotional symptoms, that we simply eradicate from awareness or minimize into irrelevance. And typically we give short shrift even to the larger problems that we can't put aside. Much as with Eddie, whose conscious system has brought him repeatedly into combative relationships, our use of denial and a battery of backup defenses seem almost boundless when dealing with our own indicators. One secondary goal of self-analysis is to help us become vigilant in discovering our defenses against admitting our indicators.

Consider an everyday sampler of defensive pretenses: A morning headache, we decide, is entirely physical; a pointless squabble with our children or spouse is entirely their doing; falling from the bottom step of the stairs was because of poor lighting. Later that same morning, there's the state of uncontrolled rage we went into when the bus driver drove away despite our calling out, and the senseless quarrel with a coworker upon arrival at the office. All along the way we keep rationalizing that everyone is at fault except ourselves. We do this because we have been taught that our faults are blameworthy rather than an acceptable part of human nature, so we deny their presence and our responsibility for them. As time goes on, and our emotional vulnerabilities crop up again and again, we have to modify our tendencies to overlook or excuse their existence. We must learn to forgive ourselves for having problems, so that we can open a door to face them—and ourselves.

Given the conscious system's preference for defensiveness, emotional issues are easy targets for denial and blame. This applies to immediate problems as well as longstanding turmoil and tendencies we have accustomed ourselves to living with over the years. Conceding these indicators asks that we confront a prolonged situation of woe that has in large measure been self-orchestrated. Who among us will find it easy to acknowledge that a job we have held for five or ten years is demeaning and far beneath our capabilities? And who is ready to face the fact that we are in a longstanding relationship or marriage that is truly studded with problems and providing very little in the way of satisfaction or support? Given the inherent difficulties of negotiating life, there is a strong likelihood that we have significant but overlooked emotional problems in work or in our relationships.

There is considerable irony to the self-analytic process. Here we are as human beings blessed with gifts of deep perception, the ability to create symbols and a representational world that expands our adaptive powers remarkably, a broad capacity for self-observation and understanding, and, above all, an array of extraordinary inner- and other-directed healing powers. And yet we blunt or deny ourselves the effective use of these gifts, especially those embodied in unconscious wisdom.

Strange indeed are the ways of nature that would require us to use special skills that our own conscious minds oppose in order to tap our most advanced ways of coping. Still, we can mobilize our self-observing function in order to keep a wary eye on our inevitable conscious defenses and conquer the defensive part of ourselves. Without this victory, we remain mired in self-defeating and self-hurtful maneuvers whose sheer pathology—still more in the way of indicators—we fail to see or acknowledge.

How, then, can we overcome these relentless defensive needs and propensities that reflect the very structure of the human mind? The answer to this nagging question lies in two great resources we all possess: the ability of the conscious mind to reflect on itself, and its capacity to comprehend, analyze, and synthesize information and meaning in order to use fully its own deep unconscious wisdom.

As human beings, we possess the gift of self-consciousness, which enables us to scrutinize our own thoughts, feelings, choices, and behaviors. Through this self-reflective process we can evaluate and even anticipate the consequences of a particular line of thought or action, and we can change our attitude or mode of reacting. But it is not simply a matter of seeing the errors of our ways and setting them straight. These self-assessing efforts are under the sway of two opposing forces: the search for insight and emotional health on the one hand and defensive and self-defeating impulses on the other.

In general, the fearful and guilty part of the mind has the greater say in our conscious evaluations and decisions. Yet the conscious mind is expert at covering over the hurtful side of our choices and at making excuses for the harm that can't be ignored. This alliance between conscious functioning and the deep unconscious fear/guilt system—that resi-

due of all that has been traumatic and terrible in our lives—
is inevitable. With much of this alliance well beyond awareness, the effects are difficult to recognize, let alone combat.

Only by adopting special forms of conscious vigilance
and by searching for indicators and making use of trigger
decoding to access the insights of the deep unconscious
system can we generate a power equal to or greater than
that of the unconscious fear/guilt system. In the end, the
conscious system can win out over our most hurtful tendencies, but it needs a lot of help to do it. And the battle
begins where we either empower ourselves to see the issues
before us or engage in the grand pretense that all's well
that blindness shows us—and pay the price accordingly.

Self-assessment is a critical aspect of every step in self-
analysis. It is a faculty that must be called forth deliberately, and it must even watch over itself to assure its
continued use. Self-scrutiny is greatly influenced by our
emotional state; in the heat of an emotional interchange or
in the midst of a vexing emotional issue, it is all too easy
to relax or lose this vital function. We must nurture and
develop the capacity for self-study, sharpen it as a tool and
value it for all it can give us. And even where we must face
and examine behaviors and feelings that disturb our sense
of equilibrium and self, maintaining an inner vigilance will
serve us far more than blunting our consciousness.

We can shore up our self-observing capacity in several
ways. First, we can learn the "tricks" foisted upon us by
our conscious selves—the shapes taken by our self-defeating
armor, our self-deceptive arguments, our many ways of
avoiding and denying, and the guileful means by which we
keep ourselves from initiating effective self-analysis. We can
also benefit from our capacity to observe others, as these
deflective devices are far easier to recognize in those around

us than within ourselves. To self-observe well, we must be prepared to see our own ills and defensiveness in those of others.

Eddie is again a case in point: His self-observing function failed him when Jan left him. Rather than turning inward to recognize his own failings and indicators, he looked outward and blamed her for almost all of his woes. To further support his self-blindness, he labored hard to discover and point out the defensiveness of his friends. If he had called forth his own self-vigilance, he could have both acknowledged his own indicators and realized that he is a lot like his friends at the club. In addition, Eddie's self-vigilance was impaired by the very emotional issues he needed to scrutinize; given his chronic interpersonal difficulties, tendencies to be sadistic, and propensity to somatize when under stress, his self-observing abilities were impaired because of the nature of his problems and their enormity. Unconsciously overwhelmed, all Eddie could do was project his impairments onto Jan and his friends and massively deny his own handicaps.

What then must we do to be incisive and up-front about the need for self-analysis? And what are the barriers we are likely to come upon in trying to motivate ourselves to engage in self-exploration?

Self-analysis is by no means a random or casual process; it is driven by emotional pain and issue. It arises from inner need and promises an exquisite answer to such needs. Thus the recognition of suffering from one or more emotional indicators/problems is the first step in self-analysis. And it is essential that we see our role in their existence and continuation and that we have a say in how a situation will turn out.

Follow Eddie's story with me now to see what I mean. Rather than confronting his indicators, he finds virtue in the disasters of his relationships by claiming that previously broken ties enable him to know quickly when things have gone awry. To crown this masterpiece of denial, he calmly plans to find someone else—not realizing that it is obvious to the rest of us that there's little chance the next relationship will be any different from its predecessors.

Next we find Eddie engaged in using the classic blame-the-other-person defense that involves both the denial of personal responsibility and the projection of blame onto the other person—a defense from which no one is immune. There is a laundry list of complaints: Jan is unbearable; Jan is a nag; Jan wants to be slapped around; Jan's a sexual tease; Jan wants to change me—and who wants that? Clearly, not Eddie. Even his own physical symptom of heartburn is laid at Jan's doorstep. There can be no change in the face of this kind of denial, nothing but repetition of the painful past.

Finally, because dozens of defensive maneuvers are never enough to suppress the truth that lies below them, Eddie resorts to insisting everyone else but he is inappropriately defensive and claiming that he's the only honest and forthright person in the crowd. In self-analysis we must learn, almost instinctively, not to trust our criticisms of others; the more vociferous our protest, the more likely we are expressing the truth about ourselves. By arming conscious vigilance with insights of this kind, we alert it to where we are likely to be resisting self-analysis and avoiding the painful truths it will reveal. If we keep remembering that we pay a price in emotional constriction and suffering for these defenses, we can enhance our motivation to break them down.

Given Eddie's lineup of defenses—denial, blaming others, projection, rationalization—there's little chance that he will turn to self-analysis to understand more fully and honestly what really went wrong in his relationship with Jan, including his own contribution to his seemingly predestined fate. The conscious system tends to perseverate, to stick to its patterns of thinking and reacting despite ample evidence that things are amiss and there must be a better way to handle everything. When it comes to survival, fixed patterns of responding are highly valuable—we really don't want to have to learn over and over again how to obtain food, where to live, and how to see the signs of impending danger. But in the emotional domain, we need greater flexibility to develop the means of facing our foibles and inadequacies so we can do something to change the way we are.

Eddie has a wide range of symptomatic indicators—interpersonal difficulties, potency problems, overdefensiveness, somatization (emotionally founded physical symptoms)—against which he has erected massive obstacles to initiating self-analysis, front-line resistance indicators. To recognize these deterrents you should carry out self-analysis at least once a day for a minimum of twenty minutes. Some people may need to develop this concentrated time of self-healing by starting out with lesser efforts—five-, then ten- and fifteen-minute periods—and building toward a twenty-minute period of self-contemplation—forty minutes being optimal. In the long run, self-analysis should help you to understand aspects of your emotional issues of which you were previously quite unaware; it should help you to see things that are invisible to the conscious mind. Should you not learn more about yourself, you should identify resistance indicators and subject them to self-exploration. In a sense, you must consciously force yourself to do something for yourself in a way that your own conscious system opposes. While simply overcoming the obstacle can help—for example, pressing forward with the process despite conscious reluctance—understanding the deeper meanings of the problem is even more useful.

Those with a strong capacity for self-vigilance recognize these obstacles to understanding ourselves at every step. The obstacles begin with denying indicators of need and extend into the process—not feeling that you have the time to sit or lie still for twenty minutes, not finding the means to collect in the mind the necessary material for self-exploration, blocking on free associating, missing the critical triggers, failing to synthesize the fragments of understanding that emerge during an effective period of processing. We will keep an eye on these resistance indicators as we develop the steps of the self-analysis effort.

With so much to overcome, we can see again why self-analysis is best done as a daily exercise, and why it is not uncommon to be faced with urgent situations that call for its more focused use. Symptomatic indicators are with us every day of our lives; they wax and wane in ways over which we often have little control. And resistance indicators lurk in the shadows ready to interfere with the self-healing process. By remaining alert to our indicators, we hand over the control of our emotional lives to ourselves.

4 ° Breaking the Defensive Barrier

WE ARE COMMITTED to doing self-analysis. What is it that stands in the way of sitting down in a comfortable armchair or lying down alone in bed so we can get going? We have already had a good sampling of the kind of clever obstacles that the conscious system sets before us when we try to assess our emotional circumstances—our symptomatic indicators. Let's take a closer look at these first-line resistances and familiarize ourselves with their more common forms so we can be on the lookout for moments when we slip into using them ourselves.

1. Denial. This obliteration of reality is the fundamental defense against recognizing that we have a problem. Often denial is buttressed by *repression*, which enables us to "forget" that a problem exists at all. With denial, we are somewhat aware of the issue but negate its impact on our lives; we fail to see the obvious. With repression we lose sight of the issue entirely; it disappears from our thoughts.

Most major emotional issues are inescapable. We avoid dealing with them mainly by denying their existence. Still, on occasion repression sets in and we have no sense at all of our concerns—even though the situation may be grave. More minor issues—a setback at work, a failing grade, a passing hurt by a friend, an emotionally charged choice— are even more easily repressed.

Examples are legion. We feel anxious but don't acknowledge it to ourselves (we're denying a symptomatic indicator). Once we do, we then fail to realize that it's the anniversary of the death of a loved one (we've been repressing a trigger). We are repeatedly fired from our job but see no culpability for the patten (we deny another symptomatic indicator). We have no recollection of a violent quarrel with someone important to us over an issue of serious concern, nor do we realize that we've been fuming about the incident for days (we're applying repression and denial to a symptomatic indicator and trigger). We know we've been hurt and are disturbed by a remark or action of someone else, but we put it aside after giving it only brief thought (we're denying a symptomatic indicator and trigger). Or we've been suffering from heartburn and depression for days but, like Eddie, we miss the depression and think of the heartburn as entirely physical (we're denying more symptomatic indicators). Also, much like Eddie, we are suffering after an emotionally upsetting incident with someone we love, but write it off as inevitable and inconsequential and deny any responsibility for what happened as well (we're denying symptomatic indicators and triggers). To get self-analysis moving, we need to resolve the resistance indicators that are mobilized by symptomatic indicators.

oooo

Glenda is a woman in her forties, divorced and living with Bart. She has been experiencing a burning sensation in the pit of her abdomen for a month, but she hasn't had it checked. It's nothing, she told Bart, I haven't been eating the right foods; or maybe it's a muscle strain from jogging, or some kind of tension. Anyhow, it will pass.

Bart has a problem with alcohol; consuming a bottle of hard liquor in an evening is routine for him. And he's not a docile drunk; he's quarrelsome at his best and physically abusive at his worst. It's in his genes, Glenda tells herself; he's going to get some therapy and change; there aren't any good men out there anyhow, and besides, I can take it, I had the same thing with my father, and I could handle him. You've got to concentrate on the good moments.

Denial and its common companions, rationalizing or making excuses and dismissing the issues, are in abundance here. Never once does Glenda think she has a physical or emotional/interpersonal problem, and if the thought were to cross her mind, it would be gone without a trace before it could have any real effect. It is extremely common to use denial when physical symptoms are first experienced, often with disastrous results. (In Glenda's case, she eventually went to a doctor who diagnosed a peptic ulcer—a common psychosomatic illness).

It is emotionally maladaptive (another indicator) to exercise sustained denial in response to ominous, persistent, or recurrent physical distress—signs of serious illness. And it is also a perilous use of denial to put aside and rationalize away notable and lasting difficulties in an emotionally important relationship. An important early goal of self-analysis is recognizing your own use of denial and casting it aside to face the truth—that you *are* suffering emotionally. Achieving this goal enhances not only the self-analysis effort itself but also the very fiber of your life.

How, then, do we safeguard against the self-defeating use of denial and repression? Again, the answer is twofold: First, we must maintain *conscious vigilance*, and be ever alert to the likelihood that we are repressing, suppressing, or denying an emotional symptom or concern. Second, we should always assume that denial is operating in our perception of ourselves and others, and make constant efforts at self-analysis to discover its presence and undo its effects. During our daily period of contemplation, we should replay each day to see what we have missed or belittled, or otherwise put aside in our emotional lives; we should list our emotional disturbances and issues in our minds, and then press harder to find the issues they cover up. We should become hunters who have no place for complacency and lack of vision, and for whom constant alertness is the credo. And remember that behind every denial, every "I'm not responsible," every "It's not my fault," there lies a full share of accountability.

2. Blaming other people and other causes. Blaming and projecting (attributing our own difficulties to others) are among the most constant companions of denial and repression. Here, of course, Eddie is again a prime example. A man who has failed repeatedly to establish a lasting and satisfying relationship with a woman entirely blames the women in his life for these failures. Who among us has not resorted to this line of self-deception and defense?

The conscious system is a storehouse for blaming devices: It's their fault, not mine (or hardly mine); life is tough, so what happened is no surprise; people are selfish, they can't

be trusted; men are rotten, women deceptive. We are prepared to see ourselves as victims far more readily than as
victimizers; the need to deny aggression and to avoid being
the guilty party seems to play a large role in that choice.

But there are still more ways of blaming others and
circumstances: Look at my parents and my childhood, no
wonder I am this way; it's the fault of human nature; things
like this are bound to happen to anyone; and to misuse the
insights of this book, I had no choice, my conscious system,
or some unconscious need beyond my control, made me
do it (disowning responsibility for your own actions by
blaming a disowned part of yourself).

Glenda used her share of blaming others in order to avoid
acknowledging and analyzing her own contributions to her
miseries. Regarding her abdominal pain, she argued that Bart
was against her going to a doctor because he didn't believe
in today's medical practices. She held her mother accountable
for her choice of Bart as a lover, claiming that she had inher-
ited her mother's fateful attraction to destructive men. And
she blamed rotten luck for the men she met throughout her
life, and Bart for not going to therapy sooner and for not
having enough self-control to stop drinking.

Familiar themes. The conscious system is exceedingly
inventive in helping us deny our helplessness and protect
our inveterate narcissism; and it is all too ready to overlook
the price we pay for blaming others rather than facing up
to ourselves. How easy it is to see the failings and hurtful
qualities of others, especially as the view blinds us to our
own vulnerabilities and nastiness. And all of us deny and
obliterate our own problems by blaming others in order to
sustain a need for suffering and punishment, or to prove
we can survive brutalities and physical illness—needs gen-
erated by the unconscious fear/guilt system.

What then is the answer to this aspect of human nature? We need another sort of conscious vigilance to be on the alert for the use of both denial and blaming others. In any situation, no matter how convinced we are of another's culpability and no matter how powerful the evidence we garner to support our case, assume that we are more responsible than not; the larger the dossier we prepare against the other person, the more likely we are covering over a major contribution of our own. The more we cry unfair and foul to the actions of someone else, the more we should feel obliged to look at ourselves in humble self-scrutiny to discover our own accountability. It is always there.

Every emotional conflict and disturbance is an interactional product—a result of a dyadic or other system—in which responsibility must be shared by all concerned, including ourselves. Even when another person has assaulted you physically, you can be almost certain that you did something to provoke the attack. Most of what you get is well deserved; find out why or you'll get plenty more of the same.

Michael is a dress manufacturer; he is married to Edna. He comes home one evening in a rage at a supplier, Danny, with whom he had a pricing arrangement that involved a substantial discount and who suddenly reneged on the deal. Michael rants and raves about Dan's treachery and how people in the industry betray him and can't be trusted. After listening for a while Edna interrupts and points out that this sort of thing happens to him again and again, while it seldom happens to his associates. With that the battle is joined: Michael feels misunderstood and attacked, Edna feels that Michael lacks insight into his own heavy-handed and provocative ways— not only in business but in their marriage.

As many of us know, there's virtually no way out of this

kind of downward-spiraling, conscious system give and take. Each person is right to some degree, and each is also wrong. And when people are hurting, they seldom are able to step back to take a hard look at themselves in order to see their own contribution to their wound—unless they're tired of being wounded and opt for self-analysis.

Just as Eddie's woes came from both himself and Jan, Michael's pain came from both himself and his supplier (Michael was every bit a conniver), and from him and Edna as well. Acknowledging the part you play in being attacked "unjustly" or in falling into an endless quarrel is far more a triumph than a defeat.

The night of this upset Michael has a dream:

He is driving his car in an alleyway when he bangs into another vehicle. The driver of the second car then bangs back into him.

It takes little in the way of associating to the dream— the other car resembled the one owned by Danny—for Michael to suddenly remember that he had completely forgotten an incident that had occurred with Danny the day before the man's phone call. Danny had driven Michael to a restaurant where they were to have lunch. During the ride, Danny had shared some personal problems with Michael—his marriage was falling apart. For some inexplicable reason (actually, Michael's conflicts about staying in his own marriage), Michael had responded rather unsympathetically, at first teasing Danny over his inability to resolve the marital crisis and then trying to goad Danny into leaving his wife peremptorily. By the time they had arrived at the restaurant, Danny was both furious with Michael and deeply depressed. On the following day Danny had called to say the old deal between them was off.

OOOO

If you are still puzzled by how Michael could have forgotten that incident, you have not yet become sufficiently well acquainted with your own conscious system and its defensive ways of coping. As for Michael, he rather quickly sees that he is the provocateur in his dream, as he was in real life. There is no escaping this insight, and Michael feels badly about what he has done; he decides to call Danny to see if he can make amends. Without self-analysis, the call would never be made.

Michael also speaks to Edna, acknowledging that the way he had spoken of the situation with Danny had been annoying, and he rather wisely avoids telling her that nonetheless she should look at her side of the quarrel as well. Michael's dream and associations lead him to realize that hostility comes in many disguised packages: Telling someone else he or she is at fault—no matter how true—is one of them.

Given her husband's conciliatory attitude, Edna responds by saying she herself had dreamed of a mob of men rampaging through the streets entirely out of control. Her own associations take her back to her father's uncontrolled drinking buddies and his bouts of violence against his wife and children. Edna recognizes her dread of controversy and disagreement and her excessive need for peace at any price. Her undue anxieties over Michael's conflict with Danny are now quite evident. In undoing denial, remarkable insights and solutions are waiting to be had on all sides—if we dare take the risk.

3. *Rationalization.* Denial and excuse making go hand in hand and often blend into blaming attitudes. Faced with an upsetting situation, we tell ourselves we needn't go into the details or the deeper levels because it will pass. We

depreciate the importance of an emotional problem, saying it really doesn't matter much, or we claim we really don't want what we can't have in the first place. We again say life is like that, or that we've just had a few bad breaks, as if the experience or anxiety were unavoidable. Or we regale ourselves with stories of our rotten childhoods and parents, denying the good experiences (at times, good things are also a threat and are denied; blaming and rationalizing depend on things being bad out there), and try to convince ourselves that there's no way we could be different.

Eddie's rationalization was that women have qualities that irritate him. Later he added that relationships are difficult; no one should be intimate with another person for more than a year or two—the strain is too great and the baggage too heavy. And when he was desperate, he invoked the seemingly unassailable defense of using the past as an excuse for his current behavior. My parents quarreled incessantly, he would wail, and they were divorced when I was seven, how could I possibly know what a good relationship is like? For Michael, the rationalization was, I really didn't mean to be hurtful to Danny, I was trying to help; besides, it was what he wanted to hear.

The memory component of the conscious system has unlimited rationalizations stored away. We must invoke conscious vigilance to safeguard against buying into our own excuses and conning ourselves into believing falsehoods, half-truths, and irrelevant whole truths that the conscious system enlists mainly to buttress defensive denial.

4. Dismissal devices. Here we dismiss or downplay insights into the presence of symptomatic indicators and reject valid points made by others who are trying to alert us to the nature of our behavior. This last is a knotty issue: On the one hand, there is a hostile, blaming element in telling someone of his or her accountability, but on the other, there is often a great deal of truth in what's being said.

Denial and avoidance have their protective value, though they do so, we must remember, at considerable cost (they have a low help/hurt ratio). No one is really eager to give up this kind of protection, especially when someone else is trying to force a person to do it. To shift from denial to facing ourselves, each person alone can and must engineer the change. We can absorb the anxiety over the temporary loss of protection (which will soon be replaced by insight and new and better ways of coping) far more easily when we direct the scenario, and when we can understand that our motives for change are truly constructive. And we alone know when we are ready to modify or give up a defense; we need to choose the right moment lest we become overwhelmed by what is then exposed. These *denial barriers* are seldom successfully assailed by anyone other than the builder.

5. *Blind action.* Taking a hard look at ourselves requires thought and contemplation. One way to preclude the effective use of self-processing is to shift into action—to engage in mindless activity or effect a hasty solution. Mostly we are acting to escape the situation; we are engaged in an action form of denial that is ultimately blind and blinding. Often we back up this kind of defensiveness with seemingly astute rationalizations: I had to take the situation into hand; after all, it's my right to decide where my life should be going; or, as Eddie said, I let her out of the situation before it destroyed me.

Many people take pride in taking action even though the act precedes rather than follows self-analysis. Our culture overvalues action and devalues the kind of contemplation that could lead to a more effective endeavor. But blind action, though it may bring momentary relief, is another denial-based solution with a low help/hurt ratio. People who tend to act before exploring deeply are likely to lead impetuous lives repeating the same mistakes indefinitely.

Bart, Glenda's boyfriend, lived a life of action—not only by drinking excessively but also by having frequent affairs and by repeatedly changing jobs. Only rarely did he sit down to reason out his choices, but even then he allowed for only conscious system rumination. In the end, this kind of thinking had little effect on his decisions, which, he'd say with pride, came from gut feelings and intuitions— certainly not from encoded wisdom.

The safeguard against these tendencies lies in being alert to all impulses to act and to all rationalizations designed to justify acting before exploring. In the emotional domain, these acts are likely to be motivated by the alliance between the conscious system and the deep fear/guilt system. Indeed, let the actor beware.

Let's go back one last time to Eddie and his social woes. After mentioning his heartburn, he changed the subject for a moment; he told an anecdote that had no direct bearing on our discussion despite its somewhat logical connection to the issues before us. Such stories are as precious for self-analysis as dreams.

Eddie said: "It's not just problems at home either. There's this new guy at work, and I hate to say it, but he's a real jerk. I mean, the guy is in some kind of blizzard and he's really been getting my goat, I'm ready to burst. He keeps making these major mistakes, but as if that's not bad enough—he's supposed to have had a lot of experience at what he's doing—he keeps saying it's not his fault. I mean, it's never his fault, there's always someone else who's to blame. I've never seen anything like it; it could drive you crazy watching him concoct excuse after excuse. And he's got this temper that antagonizes the hell out of everyone, yet he can't see what he's doing and he blames us when we react and get peeved at him. Underneath, like you guys say, he must be in a rage; he's so damn insecure, I'll bet anything he's impotent as hell. He'll never get anywhere unless he gets a handle on what he's doing."

Even if you're not acquainted yet with trigger decoding, this story is not difficult to figure out. Eddie has just been talking about his breakup with Jan—his trigger—and consciously blaming her for their distress. The story about the man at work is an encoded response to the same trigger situation. The themes in this displaced story will reveal Eddie's unconscious reactions to the situation.

This is the essence of his decoded unconscious message: I (Eddie, disguised as the new employee) am really a jerk and in a blizzard (Eddie's unconscious perceptions of himself in the situation with Jan, a rather stark though accurate appraisal). I make major mistakes and then deny them, blaming Jan for my own errors (Eddie's mistakes encoded as the new employee's errors; his unconscious realization that blaming Jan for his own foibles is wrongheaded and defensive). I am provocative and have a bad temper, but fail to see it and end up blaming Jan for what I do and am (disguised in the description of the man at work). And given all of this, I must be in a deep rage, and both insecure and impotent (Eddie's disguised self-diagnosis, and quite a good one at that). If I'm ever going to change and have a successful relationship, I must get a handle on what

I'm doing (Eddie's prescription for his own cure: Drop the denial and face yourself).

While the conscious system goes along with our resistance indicators and their denial mechanisms, the unconscious wisdom system picks up our resistances and stands opposed to their use. Self-analysis is a circular process: As we resolve resistances, we see more of the truth and have greater use of our own unconscious wisdom—the best antidote to conscious system defensiveness.

Some final points of advice: In searching for indicators for self-analysis, it seems best to take a personal approach and to rely on developing your own sensitivities to your emotional symptoms and issues. Often it is necessary to change not only psychological defenses but viewpoints that have been supported by family and culture; when you realize that you are suffering, you must turn against their support for your denial. Each family has a set of values regarding emotional ills: Where one family would see no dysfunction in a child who retreats to his room every day after school and shows no interest in having friends, another might press the child to go out and play with other children; failing that, they might soon usher him to the office of a psychotherapist.

Cultures also differ in their assessments of which behaviors or experiences are thought of as aberrant. Any number of ancient cultures accepted the murder of female infants as the norm, while others saw transvestitism as a sign of spiritual maturity because it was said to imply the transcendence of sexual distinction. Even today, some cultures see hallucinations as quite normal, while others treat them as indications of psychosis. The assessment of emotional disturbance is complicated and varies greatly among individuals. This is why we must learn to rely on ourselves to discover the presence of symptomatic indicators and the roots of our troubles.

There are many motives for using the denial package, most of them unconscious. We do not want to see ourselves as troubled or unable to cope; we prefer not to experience conflict or the guilt of choosing one person over another where someone must be hurt. We want also secretly to believe in our own omnipotence and infallibility as well as our false sense of immortality; we try to avoid emotionally painful confrontations with anxiety-provoking issues. We are reluctant to see ourselves as emotionally troubled; we prefer to think of our bodily ills as physically rather than psychologically caused. We strive also to believe that we are in control of our emotions and behaviors, denying that there are powerful forces operating beyond awareness over which we have far less control—unless we get to them through trigger decoding. And in the false glow of our self-aggrandizing narcissism, we dare not believe that we cause hurt to others or ourselves—only that we are kind and loving, and mean the best for everyone.

Against this massive pressure toward resistance and ignorance stands another set of motives emanating from the unconscious wisdom system that moves us toward the truth and the resolution of costly defenses. Decoded truths bring insights that set us free from our own self-defeating ways and allow for growth and harmony within ourselves and with others. Self-analysis is rich in its rewards.

Typically, you will pass through three phases in developing an uncompromising capacity to acknowledge your symptomatic indicators for self-analysis. First, there is a period in which there is rampant use of denial and its gang of supporters. Second, there is a transitional phase during which denial-based defenses are still automatically invoked, but there is a belated recognition of their use. Your burgeoning self-observing function becomes adept at recognizing the signs of denial and sees to it that you abandon the defense in favor of a hard look at reality. The insights that then follow allow for a gradual transition into the third phase in which the use of denial becomes almost superfluous, though occasional lapses are inevitable because of the deep imprints that habits leave on our minds. In this phase you have achieved an optimal capacity to face up to emotional vulnerabilities and issues without undue self-deception. These are the lofty heights of honesty; by this time you are ready for self-analysis.

5 ∘ Understanding Unconscious Communication

THOUGH SELF-ANALYSIS relies on spontaneity and on open and unencumbered associations, it also has its rules, tools, methods, and materials—and its moments when thoughtful analysis and synthesis must be carried out. The process is much like a game in which you become something of a poet, unraveling the metaphors of your own encoded wisdom system. The poetry translates into wise insights reflected in moments of complete surprise that follow upon the sudden realization of how a trigger-decoded insight gives integrated meaning to half a dozen previously disconnected anxieties, false moves, and unexplained dreams. It's something like entering a tunnel of loving realizations in which the uncanny, the inexplicable, and the absolutely unexpected are the mode of experience; expanded self-knowledge and emotional improvement are the prizes.

Self-analysis usually *begins* in one of two ways: either with an emotional problem that we want to resolve—a symptomatic indicator—or with a dream or other narrative, an unconscious message, that we'd like to understand. Though we speak mostly of analyzing a dream, the real power behind the self-analytic process comes from disquieting symptoms—and the triggers that provoke them.

But here's the rub: With either of these beginnings, we are actually at the *end* of the most important part of the process. That is, by the time we've experienced a symptom or remembered a dream, most of the critical events that are influencing the course of our emotional lives have already happened: We've gone through an emotional trigger experience, we've processed or worked over that experience consciously and unconsciously, and the emotional consequences of this experience and its processing have already begun to show themselves.

By the time we get around to remembering and associating to our dreams, we've already made a *conscious* assessment of our symptomatic indicators and trigger issues—if we happened to notice them. In addition, we have also most certainly arrived at definite *unconscious* conclusions— all this *before* we begin to analyze a dream. The dream is mainly an encoded intelligence report on occurrences up to the night the dream is dreamed. *Self-analysis is a way to retrace our steps in order to integrate unconscious knowledge with future action.* It is a process we carry out to discover what we've *really* been up against, what the issues really are— and a path to discovering the disguised answers to our dilemmas.

The ultimate issue that calls for self-analysis is not a dream (unless it is a nightmarish indicator itself), but *the experience of an emotionally charged trigger event*—a situation that has disturbed our emotional equilibrium and created the symptoms and other indicators that require a fresh coping response. The conscious system cannot deal with emotional issues straightforwardly—only rarely can it successfully analyze the meanings of our trigger situations so we can know *consciously* how we are reacting unconsciously. *We therefore must take a detour through self-analysis to reach these deeper answers.*

So, let's begin at the actual beginning: A trigger experience produces a symptom that is a heavily encoded maladaptive reaction to the stimulus; a dream is a more easily decoded response to the same trigger episode. To understand the structure of one is to have insight into the structure of the other. Similarly, a dream dreamed in response to an emotionally charged choice—of job, lover—shows, immediately on decoding, the unconscious meanings of the alternatives that are available to us. The sequence is always from triggers to symptoms and dreams.

Don Waring is the host of a television interview show. He is married and has a four-year-old daughter, Beth. He works evenings, while his wife, Nan, works days. It's been that way for the past three years, and, given their financial needs, there's been no evident problem; they spend weekends and vacations together and are content with the few extra hours they also share each week when their free periods overlap.

One week Don finds himself uncharacteristically anxious and angry with his wife; he keeps picking fights with her for no apparent reason. On impulse, he announces at the end of a week of carping that he's decided to go away the following weekend to visit a former colleague from his TV station. Nan has no idea of what she could have done to bring this on; Don also can't get his bearings on what he's doing. He tries making a list of his grievances against his wife; he tries to analyze his anger, but nothing makes sense. All he can come up with is that he's feeling stressed by work and that maybe he's taking out on his wife his worries about budget cuts and the possibility of losing his job.

Don is acutely aware of his symptomatic indicators and can sense that something must have set it all in motion, but aside from the office tensions, nothing comes to mind to explain his behavior. And neither consciously resolving to get himself under control nor recognizing the possible displacement from the job situation onto Nan does anything to reduce his level of anxiety or enable him to let up on his wife. His capacity for self-observation is not sufficiently developed to empower his conscious system to sort things out.

Only rarely is the critical trigger for an emotional upset immediately evident. Of course, we are more likely to recognize a trigger when the evocative issue is of major proportions, such as a vital life decision or when someone we've loved dies or is ill. But we are likely to be surprised to discover how often we forget (repress) or deny even blatant traumas. The opposition and defenses of our conscious system that take umbrage at our search for deep understanding are always with us. And when the trigger is in sharp focus, we often will have trouble coming up with the dreams and free associations we need to build a network of themes and images that will enable us to get in touch with our unconscious responses.

Don's difficulties remain shrouded in mystery until he recalls this dream:

He is being held prisoner by a man in a house; somehow he senses that his mother is responsible for what is going on.

Don is tempted first to analyze his dream without associating to it or searching for its triggers. This direct approach seems a lot easier than trying to free-associate to a dream and allowing the process to unfold from there. The guileful, unseen defensive pressures of our conscious system draw us inevitably to the immediate surface of a dream; free-associating to a dream is a less natural approach, even though its potential yield for insight is far greater than any frontal assault.

Going for the obvious, Don thinks about his mother, who lives in another city. She is, he thinks, a fairly nice woman—he's had no feeling that she's been hurtful in any way, no sense that she's trying to entrap him or, to use the Freudian dream-wish notion, that he wishes to be her captive.

Looking directly at a dream without considering the sequence of events to which it belongs, and without a sense of its disguised meanings and adaptive value, is much like taking a single photograph of an already-repaired site of a hurricane. You will find only a few signs of the ruination, and there's no notion of the process that led to the devastation.

The deep unconscious wisdom system can speak to us only through displaced narratives and images. The system creates the dream to inform us of its understanding, but its most critical messages are nonmanifest. If Don has an emotional issue with his mother, he is likely to dream of his wife, or of a friend's mother, or of someone else on Mother's Day. As a rule, he cannot and will not dream directly of the person with whom he has the most intense unconscious conflicts. Whatever the underlying conflicts between Don and his mother, we can be quite certain that she is not the center of his unconscious conflicts at the moment. To find out who this person is, and what the conflict is about, we need his associations to the dream.

While the dream itself is a disguised reaction to an earlier trigger, it functions best as a point of departure for free associations. Free associations move out from the manifest (surface) dream into new scenes, with people who are different from those in the direct dream images and, often, into different time frames as well. And the themes of these evoked stories will lead us back to the trigger for the dream; they will also tell us what we need to know about those trigger experiences.

Don's first association is to a story he'd read about a man who died trapped in a burning building. His thoughts drift next to the events of the day of the dream. There had been a breaking news story at the television studio, and Don had been called that day at home to see if he could come in to help with the coverage. Don had had to say no, because there was no one with whom he could leave his daughter. He had felt a bit annoyed; he was concerned about job stability and the chance that his work on the story could help him move into the news bureau where he could do the morning news. He shrugged off his disappointment by rationalizing that it would mean getting up long before dawn; besides, his daughter had made a lovely cutout of a father and child and had interrupted his thoughts to give it to him. At pleasant moments like that, there was no sense carping about caring for Beth; she gave a lot back for the little effort and sacrifice it took.

The bridging themes in Don's dream associational network point again to the idea of entrapment, which is now, through the associations to the dream, connected with death. A possible trigger for the dream has also been introduced: the invitation that Don had had to refuse. His conscious system had accepted the reality of the situation and quickly dropped the subject. But not his deep unconscious wisdom system. To clarify further and find the solution to his symptomatic behaviors, Don needed to generate more associations to his dream, and that's exactly what he did.

Don next recalls an interview he had carried out three nights earlier that had touched him emotionally. It was with a Vietnam veteran who had been held prisoner by the Vietcong for four years. In his mind, Don goes over many of the horrible tales of torture and deprivation the man had told.

There was the prisoner theme again. And the breaking news story, now that Don thinks about it, was about the release of an American held hostage in Lebanon. A *coalescing network* was developing—an associational complex with identifiable recurrent and interrelated themes.

In light of these associations, Don begrudgingly acknowledges that maybe he does feel a bit confined by his family. He had never consciously thought of it as imprisonment, but then again, he begins to wonder now.

Don's thoughts turn back to his mother. He remembers an incident he had witnessed as a child of perhaps four or five in which his parents had quarreled violently and his mother had locked herself in the bathroom, only to have trouble getting out when things cooled down.

Continuing his alternation between free-associating and analyzing/synthesizing, Don notices that here, entrapment is associated with a marital quarrel. Hadn't his wife called his mother the other day and told her about Don's recent irritations? Weren't the two of them as thick as thieves? Was Don's wife being disguised as his mother? And was she the one behind his imprisonment?

Suddenly Don remembers an incident from two weeks earlier. How could he have forgotten it? His daughter had developed a fever and Don had taken her to the pediatrician. Though it was late in the afternoon, the doctor's office was overcrowded. Don was delayed beyond his expectations and he actually missed the first part of an interview he had been scheduled to do. He had called in and arranged for a replacement, and his boss had been quite understanding. Nevertheless, Don was annoyed that, when he called Nan to ask her to help out, she said she was about to go into an important meeting and just couldn't get away from her job. With a shudder, Don now realizes that the man whose interview he had missed had been involved in a mercy killing of his wife.

Consciously, Don felt a great deal of love for his daughter and wife, whatever his resentments. All this is true, but it's only part of the story. The conscious system is in general mild in its approaches to emotional issues. Given the fact that we often consciously experience rather vengeful and seductive thoughts and fantasies, this relative meekness becomes apparent only when conscious themes are compared with those we garner through decoding the messages from our deep unconscious wisdom system. There we discover a disarmingly strong degree of bluntness and harshness; evidently, on this deep and relatively nondefensive level, we experience the world in ways that are primitive and crude by our usual, conscious standards. This is one of the reasons we consciously abhor decoding: We become privy to very disconcerting reactions to our emotional triggers; and we tend to feel so guilty that we fail to realize that this is human nature in the raw. We push these rough perceptions of ourselves and others into the unconscious part of the mind before we are aware that they exist.

These unconscious responses and images control our emotional lives. Look at Don: Triggered by frustrations connected with his having to care for his daughter, he comes under the sway of powerful unconscious perceptions of being imprisoned, which are experienced as life threatening. He reacts unconsciously to this situation with murderous feelings of his own. With all of these stirrings operating outside of awareness, he becomes uncontrollably hostile toward his wife and uncharacteristically plans to leave for a weekend. In light of Don's unconscious feelings, these seem to be reasonable compromise behaviors. But, were he to remain unaware of his unconscious processing, he could well be headed toward a divorce. With the underlying issues beyond awareness, there is little he could do to alter this course. Decoding is his most rational way out of this bind.

There is a lot now to convince Don that he feels entrapped. Suddenly he recognizes the man in his dream: He is the husband of a woman who had baby-sat for their daughter soon after she was born. The couple had divorced and left the area; Don had not thought of them in years.

All of his efforts at conscious probing had brought only frustration without fresh insight. Yet, by associating to and decoding his dream, Don was able to extract precious understanding from his encoded wisdom system. While consciously Don's obligation to take care of his daughter was nothing more than a minor irritant, unconsciously it was an entrapment that promised annihilation. Manifestly, Don was also seemingly at peace with his wife (until recently), but unconsciously he was at war with her—as his parents had been in his childhood. The contrast between the two forms of self-knowledge is quite evident.

Finally, encoded in the deep unconscious wisdom system's communications is a viable solution to Don's conflict that was not available to him through conscious deliberations: hire a baby-sitter (encoded in the identity of the man who was holding him prisoner). Because Don and his wife were both consciously convinced that they couldn't afford a sitter, they had set aside that particular option more than a year earlier. Armed with his dream and his decoded insights, and no longer unconsciously driven to be angry with his wife, Don proposed to hire a sitter once again—and they soon did. Don canceled his plans to go away—he really didn't like the man he was going to visit anyway (had he been up to a bit of self-punishment?). Effective self-analysis has these kinds of salutary effects.

What, then, are the steps through which a dream or other encoded narrative is *created*? I would propose the following:

1. *The experience of an emotionally charged trigger.* Self-analysis is about discovering triggers—the decisions and traumas that disturb our emotional equilibrium. Dreams facilitate this search and are a vehicle for understanding; they contribute encoded themes of their own and serve to stimulate meaningful associations. Indicators—signs of emotional tension and disturbance—and dreams are both responses to *trigger experiences*; the two are equivalent, and both follow upon trigger experiences. Triggers come first in time, even though they are often recognized last in the course of self-analysis.

2. *Conscious processing.* Some aspects of trigger situations are always worked over consciously to some degree, although this work is not a major aspect of dream formation. This level of response is limited, but a conscious perception may help to shape a manifest dream—we often dream of an event that occurred during the day. Conscious processing shouldn't be trusted, but it also shouldn't be discarded entirely. We should use our conscious system and its observing and analyzing functions to the fullest, while mindful that it touches on only a small part of the story.

3. *Unconscious processing.* This is the job of the encoded wisdom system, though it includes the arousal of deep fears and guilt and the repressed memories connected to them as well; they are the most powerful source of our dream images. While the fear/guilt system has the ear of the conscious system and therefore a strong say in how we react to emotional triggers, the wisdom system controls our *communicative outlets* (what we dream and how we associate to the dream). This orchestrates the selection of stories and memories. It also controls the creation of dreams and other narratives that convey unconscious perceptions and, to a lesser extent, unconscious fantasies or daydreams, that tell us the most about our inner reaction to a trigger situation. All of this processing occurs silently and without awareness.

At times we know nothing of this because no encoded messages are produced; at other times encoded reports on this unconscious processing are made available through our dreams and displaced stories. Because of differences in how each of us reports out on the activities of our deep wisdom system, it is helpful to separate the actual unconscious processing from the disguised report on the results of this processing—the encoded dream.

Life moves from triggers to symptoms and dreams, from experience to encoded message. Decoding reverses this sequence, moving from dreams and associations back to triggers in order to illuminate symptoms—indicators. With this in mind, let's now move to the process of self-analysis and follow its course from dream to moment of insight.

6 ○ Getting Started: The Encoded Message

WE ARE NOW ready to *do* self-analysis. To get started, we must insure one function that will oversee the entire process: *conscious vigilance.* As the overseer of our emotional life and our efforts to better comprehend its underlying issues, self-observation has many tasks to carry out. We have already seen its importance in recognizing indicators, the emotional issues that drive this operation. This same observing function must keep watch over how we engage in the process moment by moment. We must learn to develop a rhythm: one moment deep in remembering and associating, the next in stepping back and taking stock of what we are doing.

Self-observation relies on an inner map of the attributes of effective self-exploration and centers on two tasks. The first involves safeguarding the exploratory process itself by keeping a watchful eye for resistances—alerting us to when we're wandering off the path to self-understanding. The second consists of keeping track of the material or contents that emerge in the course of the self-analytic effort—the indicators, triggers, and encoded messages that must eventually be synthesized into a moment of insight—and change. Ultimately self-observation sees to it that something meaningful occurs in the course of exploring and working things over. *Resistance and meaning:* These are the two foci of self-awareness.

Where to begin the process? Indicators drive the effort, but are they the best place to begin? We want to define the unconscious factors that cause our emotional tensions. The goal is to understand an aspect of our emotional lives that cannot be fathomed through conscious deliberation alone. We are out to master the unconscious powers that propel our emotional decisions and strains; we intend to expand our awareness and not to trade in the self-evident.

As we get started, should we begin the process by focusing directly on our motives for doing self-analysis in the first place? Will thinking about our emotional symptoms and pending decisions move us toward the depths we hope to plumb?

Probably not; the target for insight seldom reveals its own underpinnings. If we try to initiate self-processing this way, very likely we'll become bogged down in thinking about our ills and issues, speculating as to what they might mean. We'll be caught up in a conscious system exercise that will actually preclude the development of the narrative material needed for encoded insight. Listing and examining indicators easily distract us from the in-depth analysis we need. Indicators should be quickly identified at the outset of self-analysis and then tucked away until we develop a full communicative network that will enable us to discover their *unconscious* basis.

oooo

Arthur, a married insurance broker in his forties, feels anxious all week; he can't get rid of the tension, so he decides to analyze straight out why he feels the way he does. He lists his indicators: He's been anxious and depressed, and recently he's been unpleasant to his wife, Wendy, continually bugging her to clean up the least disorder at home. He's also had repetitive fantasies that she is having an affair with someone; this is not her style, nor is he the suspicious type, but he can't get rid of the annoying notion.

Lists of indicators tell us what's bothering us, but little more. They lead us in circles but don't reveal the compelling, deeper sources of our emotional woes. We need a more indirect attack.

So if listing and examining our indicators is not the way to get a self-analysis session moving, will listing and exploring our triggers do it? This approach requires us to make an inventory of emotionally charged experiences that may have caused the existing indicators. Does seeing that one thing causes another constitute a valid way of getting at the roots of our emotional issues? Let's allow Arthur to help us find the answer.

Arthur's indicators lead him to look at his current life situation and to enumerate some of the things that have been disturbing him lately. He's been under a lot of pressure on his job: There's a proposal whose deadline he isn't going to be able to meet; corporate insurance plans he created have turned out to have major problems; and there have been tensions between himself and his section head and some stimulating but guilt-provoking seductiveness between himself and one of the female agents. For the moment, these are all of the triggers he can find.

This is an impressive but not unusual list of possible sources of anxiety and depression. They even hint that Arthur's problems with his wife stem from his guilt about being attracted to another woman. Any or all of these trigger situations might be causing his discomfort. But how is he to know which ones?

In telling himself that these are the roots of his problem, what has Arthur really learned? That tensions and conflict make him anxious, as do job pressures and guilt over coveting a woman other than his wife? That's hardly surprising. The apparent logic and simplicity of this kind of conscious system thinking lulls us into believing we've arrived at profound answers. According to this formulation, all Arthur would need to do to find some relief from his anxiety and guilt is mobilize his resources to meet his pending deadlines, straighten out his insurance stock portfolios, make peace with his boss, and stop flirting with the other agent.

These are seemingly reasonable solutions, and they may prove somewhat helpful. But they assume that there is no unconscious driving force that put Arthur in this situation to begin with. Few problems in life are without deeper emotional reverberations. And therein lies the source of repetitive symptoms and hurtful actions that we vow to stop or change, only to find that we cannot willfully alter them.

There is a commonly misunderstood difference between *realistic danger*, where the threat is direct, and *"neurotic"* or *unrealistic danger* where the sources of disturbance are internal and based on unconscious perceptions and fantasies rather than real threat. In the first situation, the reaction is one of *fear*, a response that is in keeping with the actual situation; in the second, the reaction is one of *anxiety*, a response that goes well beyond the dangers of the external situation. Anxiety is a response to psychological danger, a response to the seeming irrational and to veiled issues; Arthur does not seem to have identified his sources of this level of disturbance.

The inadequacies of listing triggers as a way of starting self-analysis are borne out when Arthur tries to correct his problems and is only partly successful in keeping his promises to himself; though a few issues are resolved, the main indicators continue unabated. In fact, Arthur is especially bothered by the fact that establishing clear limits on his relationship with the other agent did not lessen his carping with and fantasies about his wife. His self-observing function tells him he needs something more to get himself under control; where is it to come from?

Arthur decides to press harder with his trigger list; what else has been disturbing him of late? Perhaps being more specific will help, and this time he will see what he can analyze about the triggers as well.

He'd had several quarrels with his boss over the past few weeks; one had occurred on the day before Arthur made up this second list. This leads him to think about his problems with authority figures and about his domineering father; Arthur had resolved to resist authoritarianism whenever he could. The female insurance agent had come onto him again the day before, and he had made it clear that he was no longer interested in her. This brings up his mother's seductiveness with him and her tendency to favor him over his angry, cold father; from there, his thoughts go to his past difficulties in maintaining his commitment to his wife. Is he attracted only to unavailable women and turned off by women like his wife, who is an appropriate partner for him?

Here too we see the conscious system at work, making a new list, using its memory, its bits and pieces of analytic knowledge and jargon, its ability to speculate—and its way of missing the key points entirely. Without narratives, triggers seem to tell us very little.

Frustrated and still suffering, Arthur remembers a dream one morning:

> There's a man driving a car down a highway at breakneck speed. He's being pursued by two police cars. He's robbed a bank and is trying to make his getaway.

Associating to this dream brought Arthur closer to the key trigger for his uneasiness than did all of his conscious deliberations. In allowing his thoughts to wander about in response to the dream, Arthur eventually comes to the entirely overlooked fact that in recent months he'd been lifting money from the company's petty cash account and making false entries in the books; he'd also been involved in some marginal and possibly illegal insurance deals where accusations of kickback payments might well be justified—he hadn't bothered to check out the relevant regulations. A few additional associations to several men he knew on Wall Street who had been indicted for stock frauds made clear that his encoded wisdom system knew very well that these activities were illegal. And an association to a movie about a reformed criminal encoded Arthur's unconscious advice about how to handle these dealings.

Arthur had missed entirely the actions that were causing his anxieties when he listed and examined his indicators and triggers. He also managed consciously to deny the criminality of what he was doing, rationalizing that his company owed him money and that marginal deals were not illegal deals. The denial made it impossible for Arthur effectively to exercise his self-observing function and to suspect the real source of his inner disquietude. Only now, in light of the newfound trigger and his dream and associations, could Arthur begin to grasp the *unconscious* basis of his anxiety and depression, and his reactions to his wife—he had projected his own dishonesty and problems onto her. The depths were beginning to show through.

Arthur's experience is prototypical: Deep insight came only after he remembered a dream and allowed himself to free-associate to its images. In principle, self-analysis must begin with the recollection or creation of an *origination narrative—a storied vehicle that can serve as a point of departure for free associations.* Only through storied communication can the voice of the encoded wisdom system speak and be heard.

Let's imagine now that you have settled into bed and are ready for some self-analysis. You clear your mind of the day's concerns and cast about for an origination narrative to get things going. In the back of your mind, where your self-observing function is quietly at work, you realize that you'll be starting at the end of a process that began with a trigger or two that you'll get to later on. You also know that somewhere there are several indicators you want to understand in depth.

But for starters, you relax and allow that first story to come to mind. Most of the time, this will mean remembering a dream from the previous night—one that you already recalled or that occurs to you at this very moment. Then with dream in hand—note: I mean *mental* registration; writing down dreams or other narratives greatly inhibits the freedom essential to this kind of processing—you are ready to continue.

Suppose you can't remember a dream. What other kinds

of narratives can you draw from? This question is important not only because there will be times that you will want to do self-analysis and can't remember a fresh dream (old dreams may sometimes work, but current dreams work best), but because other kinds of narratives may occur to you early in your self-analysis. As origination narratives, these stories are every bit as valuable as dreams; they are a great resource you do not want to waste.

You can use any of four classes of origination narratives to initiate self-analysis.

1. Dreams and daydreams. The most common types of origination narratives are dreams and daydreams or conscious fantasies. The stories and images that occur any time during sleep are commonly referred to as *dreams*; similar images that occur when you are awake are called *daydreams* or *fantasies*. Both are useful origination narratives.

In principle, there is no way of knowing what lies ahead once you've remembered a story. Some dreams will set off a process that leads to powerful encoded insights, while others will take you into the muddied waters of unresolvable resistances. Perhaps the only rule of thumb is that the ideal dream is of short to moderate length; long dreams tend to be difficult to process. If you conjure up any extended origination narrative, do not wander aimlessly in associating to its many elements but try to confine yourself to one segment of the story at a time. Such a tactic may well defeat the resistances that led you to produce too much encoded material for any mind to handle effectively.

A number of issues arise in trying to remember dreams or to register daydreams. The very capacity of dreams to carry and evoke deep encoded meaning makes them, and encoded narratives in general, dangerous to the conscious system. We therefore prefer to shrug off our dreams as meaningless gibberish or to intellectualize about their possible meanings and avoid associating to their images. We prefer superficial to deep messages and meanings. By being vigilantly alert to these likely resistances, we can safeguard against them.

What then favors the recall and holding on to dreams? The answer begins with awakening slowly and allowing yourself time to lie in bed before getting up and turning to the realities of the coming day. Let the dream come to you; if need be, chase after a fragment that comes through and try to expand on its contents. Don't be concerned if the dream is in pieces or brief; short dreams will often generate rich associations and a very successful self-analytic experience. And if you don't recall a dream on a particular morning—or ever—there are other narrative forms to turn to.

Holding on to a living and viable dream means not writing it down, but letting it enter the flow and ebb of your real and mental lives so that it becomes part of an ever-changing adaptive process through which you freely and actively cope with the emotional world and its vicissitudes. In principle, self-analysis is a living and evolving spontaneous process whose freedom is impaired by recording any aspect of its transactions; if you are tempted to write down any part of the experience, invoke self-vigilance and warn yourself that this is a resistance that should not be carried out. The impulse to record should be taken as a resistance indicator for unrecorded self-exploration.

To fix a dream in your mind for recall later when time will permit you to engage in the self-analytic process, first allow yourself to catch all of the dream you can recover;

then do some immediate free-associating—allowing the dream images to evoke new, yet related images and stories—before the dream recedes. These added images will often help you to secure the dream in your mind for later and more extensive processing. Briefly identifying one or two emotional triggers from the previous day or two that seem connected to the dream imagery also facilitates holding on to dreams. Triggers are good markers for dream contents; they're so intimately connected to the themes of a dream that they're like fishing lines that enable you to reel back into awareness dreams that have been submerged during the day. In general, remembering triggers proves easier than remembering dreams—even though one usually leads to the other.

We've already seen how dreams serve as origination narratives. Let's look for the moment at a daydream that served this purpose.

Cory is a young single man who attends college. One afternoon, as he is sitting in the library with a chemistry book in front of him, he has the following daydream:

He is a major league baseball player and has developed a new pitch that is impossible for batters to hit. In his first season he wins fifty-two games, but the league goes into turmoil. A group of owners secretly offers him $20 million to retire. He adamantly refuses but has a miserable winter. In the spring, he finds that the pitch no longer works; when his team discovers that he's unable to win, he's not only dropped from the roster, but he's also accused of having doctored the ball illegally. Though there's no proof, he finds himself totally humiliated and in disgrace.

Cory decides to engage in self-analysis in the quiet of the library. He wonders if the daydream has anything to do with the problem he's been having studying lately; uncharacteristically, he's failed two exams. Even though he wants to free-associate, he can't resist the temptation to think of the daydream as a compensatory fantasy. But why the failure and disgrace at the end? Does he wish to punish himself as well?

Cory knows a lot about deep self-analysis, so his self-observing function warns him that this conscious system analysis is getting him nowhere. If he wants to really find out why he's not able to study, then he'd better take a less direct approach and free-associate to the daydream.

He likes baseball, and he's the second baseman for the school's junior varsity team. He struck out with the bases loaded the other day and felt lousy; was that an important trigger? Probably not, though again it shows how the daydream is fulfilling different compensatory wishes. Try another tack, he advises himself.

One of his uncles own a small piece of a major league team. Cory's always dreamed of playing in the big leagues, though he's beginning to see that he's probably not good enough to make it. The guys on the team have been bugging him lately, and the first baseman has been downright nasty. Some of the girls at school come to watch the games and there's one he's really attracted to; he hasn't had the courage to talk to her yet. He'd sure like to make a pitch to her.

At this point, there's an unexpected breakthrough, a change in the tone of Cory's imagery from light to serious—a sign of movement. Cory suddenly thinks of another uncle with whom he had stayed during spring break. His daughter, Emily, Cory's cousin, is also in her late teens and very attractive. She and Cory had gotten involved one night in some sex play, and they would have had intercourse, but Cory lost his erection. The incident had bothered him. The next day they talked about what had happened and vowed to not get into that kind of situation again. Over the ensuing weeks, Cory had pretty much thought it out and put it all aside; but given his daydream, it was now clear that the experience was still bothering him—it was a leftover trigger for his daydream.

With that realization, the immediate trigger for the fantasy also occurred to him: Last night Cory had tried to seduce a woman who was the girlfriend of one of his fraternity brothers. He had used a host of rationalizations for the involvement—they are not engaged; he'd do it with a girlfriend of mine—but only at the last minute did they decide not to go back to her room to go to bed together. The contemporary trigger had undoubtedly stirred up the earlier experience with his cousin.

Unconscious guilt induces us to become "criminals" and leads us to punish ourselves through such means as failing school. Cory could also see by looking at his daydream that he had encoded his behavior with his cousin as a quest for infallible power (the unhittable pitch)—a need, he now realizes, that had been triggered by a serious illness in his father that had mobilized Cory's fear of loss (undone magically by the liaison with a cousin) and his own death anxieties.

Cory had now captured in awareness a series of decoded realizations that could help him to resolve his unconscious guilt and recover his ability to study. For once, being distracted from his books had paid off.

2. Marginally related or out-of-context stories. We've already met up with this type of origination narrative in chapter 4 when Eddie changed the subject of our discussion from his relationship with Jan to his situation at work.

Marginally related stories involve a change in subject, a shift to another time and/or place and to people other than those at issue. These offhand narratives usually have some logical connection to the main contents of the dialogue. At times the tale concerns an incident that the storyteller intended to mention all along, yet it still encodes important unconscious meanings.

The special value of these stories lies in their immediate connection to the triggers that evoked them in the first place. A dream occurs at night and works over the events of the prior day, and is remembered, as a rule, the following morning; there is therefore considerable time between the trigger for a dream and its moment of creation—and a lot can happen in twelve hours.

But with a marginally related story, the trigger is the immediate issue and the encoded narrative bursts through as a coping response; all that is needed are some free associations and decoding to have a powerful sense of the unconscious issues fueling the debate. And as conscious system arguments almost never get resolved, getting hold of the unconscious issue that is driving the battle can bring a kind of resolution to the situation that is impossible to reach in any other way.

Whatever the surface rationalization for bringing up a marginally related story, you should treat it as you would a dream—associate to it and take the current situation as a main trigger for the imagery and themes contained in it. This kind of self-analysis offers an immediate window into unconscious issues and into the nonmanifest, nonconscious world of experience. Analyzing these stories is an excellent way of getting to see the difference between conscious and unconscious processing.

An especially touchy situation arises when one party to an emotionally charged disagreement tells an out-of-context story in the form of a dream. Such a communication is loaded with encoded meanings that typically are beyond the awareness of both parties. In a way, these are danger-ous messages: The teller doesn't know what he or she is conveying to the listener, while the listener is reacting to strong unconscious meanings without knowing what they are. Emergency trigger decoding is the only way you can develop decoded insight into what has been conveyed—and why.

Ben is a psychologist who has joined me in a research proj-ect through which we have been investigating, through the use of mathematical models, the deep laws of emotional communication. He and the mathematician with whom we are working were to speak about our work; their audience was to be a group of hard scientists who teach at a distant university. On the day of the presentation the mathemati-cian called Ben to tell him that he was ill and Ben would have to go alone. Given his limited knowledge of mathe-matics, and the qualifications of the audience he was to address, Ben was nervous about what lay ahead.

At the presentation, Ben looked for a way to break the ice; quite spontaneously, he began with a story. "I am re-minded," he said to the group before him, "of the first meet-ing I ever attended at the Academy of Science—and it was not so long ago. A reporter spoke on forensic medicine and discussed the case of a chemist accused of dismembering his girlfriend's body; the man had disappeared before he could be apprehended and brought to trial. I had nervously raised my hand during the discussion period," Ben contin-ued, "and said something about the unconscious factors in a crime of that kind. The chairman of the panel, a well-known physicist, interrupted me and said, 'I'm sorry, Ben, we never use that word "unconscious" in these hallowed halls—never.'

"You see," Ben pointed out to his listeners, "I know what you all think of psychoanalysis and how loose and unscientific it is, but I'm here because I agree with you and I'm part of a research team that is trying to change that state of affairs."

Ben's conscious rationalization for telling this anecdote is self-evident: He wanted to let these scientists know that he's not a naive, uninformed ignoramus-psychotherapist, but someone more sophisticated and aware of how his audience thinks about him and the material they expected him to offer. It was his implied way of saying, Hey, I'm one of your group—or at least, I'd like to be, so go easy on me and listen; I may have something interesting to say.

On the conscious level, then, this out-of-context story was deliberately designed to allay Ben's conscious anxieties. But the narrative itself shows that Ben was struggling with even more powerful unconscious anxieties. He had no idea of his double motives until immediately after he had told his tale. To get in touch with his unconscious anxieties and perceptions of the situation, Ben had only to look at the surface tale: A chemist—a scientist—dismembers and murders his girlfriend. Even as he spoke, Ben was able to extract the themes from the surface narrative about the scientist-killer and transpose them into the trigger situation—the immediate setting in which he was speaking.

Ben rather quickly realized that unconsciously he was frightened to death of his audience—he was convinced that they were going to mutilate and murder him. In part, these beliefs were based on subliminal perceptions of some remarks these scientists made to Ben before he began to speak. And in part, these feelings stemmed from Ben's own inner vulnerabilities. Nonetheless, it is clear that a global and diffuse conscious anxiety expressed and masked a specific unconscious bodily anxiety. Together they threatened Ben's equilibrium.

Despite the primitive quality of these unconscious anxieties and images, Ben was comfortable as he spoke and actually made a presentation that was well received. Ben's very capacity to encode and communicate his unconscious perceptions and anxieties was an adaptive way of dealing with his underlying issues; often just remembering a dream or telling a story—activating our symbolic capacity—offers a measure of relief that simply does not occur if the channels for symbolic/encoded expression are closed off. In addition, his ability to trigger-decode some key unconscious meanings was especially helpful.

In terms of the unconscious selection involved in thinking of this story to tell his audience, we can see that Ben invoked both displacement (a change in place and person) and symbolization (disguise) in opting for this tale. The raw unconscious perceptions involve intense danger to himself at the moment; the narrative concerns the girlfriend of a chemist, and another time and place as well. The anxieties about being criticized, attacked verbally, and thought a fool are transformed (symbolized/encoded) as a physical danger that threatened Ben's body and life (clearly, his life was not in real danger).

The solution proposed by the deep unconscious wisdom system is, however, questionable: Get out before they bring you to trial and execute you. Here Ben's internal vulnerabilities overstate the danger and underestimate his resources to cope. An associated narrative presented a different option: It involved an unjustly accused criminal who stood his ground and vindicated himself against the condemnation of others. Here, the deep wisdom system offers cooler and more effective advice: Stay on and vindicate your position. This is exactly what Ben did.

Ben later associated to his father, who was a butcher, and to early incidents in his father's butcher shop, including a serious injury to his father's left hand that Ben happened to witness. Here we have a genetic—early childhood—source of Ben's translation of his own anxieties into bodily concerns; the recollection also contains allusions to the subliminally perceived violence Ben saw in his father.

The value of the self-analytic process is evident in its preventive value in Ben's case. Before the lecture, no matter how Ben tried to apprise himself of his anxieties, he was unable to get in touch with his deeper concerns. Had his ignorance continued, Ben might have felt his slaughter was beginning in response to a question or issue that conveyed nonmanifest meanings; he would have become anxious and unable to function properly. Self-analysis is the best means of preventing this kind of unconscious resonance and its consequences. Often it is possible, as it was with Ben, to carry out a brief piece of self-analysis when under emotional stress; the resultant insight can be invaluable.

3. Stories created by or about other people. The creations and lives of others contain many potential origination narratives. The possibilities include movies, television shows, novels, other works of fiction and books, plays, new stories, nonfiction writings, incidents in the lives of other people you know. Often such material comes up in the course of free-associating to another origination narrative, but there are times when you settle into the self-analytic mode and one of these narratives captures your attention. When this happens, you should conjure up the entire story and treat it as you would a dream. If the images haunt you, or if you've been overreacting to a small incident, it is likely there is a personal emotional trigger lurking behind the remembered narrative. This is a good place to initiate self-analysis.

Abby is a young, single woman in her mid-twenties; she's been riveted to her television set, preoccupied with a news story about a young child trapped in a well into which she had fallen. Through self-observation Abby realizes that she's overinvolved with the story, and she decides to do some self-analysis using the incident as her origination narrative. Once she's settled into her chair in her living room, she begins to free-associate to the story. She thinks of a series of memories from her childhood related to visits she had made with her family to relatives who owned a farm; they had a well and they often warned her to not lean over too far to look down its opening.

The aunt who ran the farm had been divorced three times; she was the kind of woman who every now and then just took off for Europe and disappeared for a few months, leaving the farmhands to handle everything. In those days, that was pretty adventurous for a woman to do, and Abby admired her for it—even though she'd often wonder why her aunt couldn't ever settle down. From there, it was an easy step for Abby to think about her engagement of two weeks; she'd already had several quarrels with her fiancé, Adam, and just two days ago she had threatened to break off the engagement.

Though there is more to the network that Abby wove around this origination narrative, there was enough here for her to realize that unconsciously she was experiencing getting married as a life-threatening entrapment. Abby now remembers a dream she'd had the night before: A man wearing a gold wedding ring was trying to smother her with a pillow. This encoded image gave strong confirmation to Abby's analytic work and insight; it's the kind of encoded confirmation that should crop up toward the end of a solid piece of self-exploration.

4. Stories you create yourself. The fictions you create are also very much like day- or sleep dreams. Whenever you settle into the self-analytic frame of mind and cannot recall an origination narrative, *you should turn inward and create a short story.* Manufacture a dream equivalent on the spot. Keep these narratives brief or there will be too much to associate to; and like Lois, who I referred to in chapter 2 and who wrote a short story about an internist and two women, take your creation once it's finished and treat it as a dream. You should never lack an origination narrative; simply overrule your own resistances when they say there's nothing to work on and see to it that you create an imaginative beginning.

Origination narratives abound in everyone's daily lives; we need only to have enough self-vigilance to capture and use them in the service of self-exploration. With narrative in mind, we've got the process started; now we're ready to free-associate.

7 ° Free-associating

THOUGH YOUR THOUGHTS can go in many directions once you've remembered an origination narrative, experience has shown that unencumbered associating to its elements should be the next step. This needn't imply rigid adherence to the associating effort; if an indicator or trigger pops into mind, make a mental note of it, but then use your self-vigilance and knowledge of the phases of self-analysis to move back into the associational mode. The associations to a dream or other origination narrative bring forth the richest source of encoded information. *Dreams are not dreamed to be analyzed but to be associated to.*

Before you get to your triggers, you must allow for a free flow of supplementary narratives and images in order to build a *dream/associational network* that will speak candidly from the encoded wisdom system. Narratives and themes flow far more loosely before we focus on our emotional triggers than they do after the triggers have been identified. Placing trigger recognition before associating tends to shift our attention to surface issues and to promote conscious system speculation about trigger experiences; this defeats the search for unconscious expressions.

Many people become anxious at the idea of free-associating to a dream (for purposes of exposition, I'll use dreams, though similar principles apply to any type of origination narrative). For some it seems extreme or antiquated. For others there's a mistaken feeling that it's a detour, while still others complain that it's hard to know what free-associating means and how to do it. Is anything we think of after remembering a dream a free association, or must the thought or image take a particular form? The answer is yes and no: Anything you think about after an origination narrative is, in the widest sense, an association to that narrative, but some associations are far more productive than others.

Free-associating originated with Freud, but many therapists today shy away from allowing their patients to associate; they prefer to work with a manifest dream and its evident implications, bypassing decoding entirely. They have lost a vital art. The manifest or surface contents of a dream per se lack available encoded meaning; they are directly stated meanings that all too often are treated as such. This is different from stating that *the manifest contents of a dream or other origination narrative contain encoded or disguised messages*. This latter proposition implies a need to *decode* manifest contents rather than work with surface connotations.

Free associations come after a dream and are often unexpected and naive; they are also further removed from the disturbing trigger experience than the manifest dream. For these reasons, they tend to convey less defended, more powerful messages than the dream itself. In most instances, the most compelling and meaningful narrative/thematic material in a dream/associational network comes in the free associations to a dream or other origination narrative. They are at the heart of self-analysis.

Free-associating is sometimes difficult and is often the source of resistance and anxiety precisely because of the power behind the images it generates. The conscious system tries to discourage the development of deep meaning in the course of self-analysis; not free-associating for any reason reflects conscious system defensiveness. Vigilance again plays a critical role in detecting these deterrents to effective exploration, and self-analysis can be used to reveal their underlying motives.

You can do most anything in response to a manifest dream, from ignoring it to interpreting its meanings at face value. Often you will think of added dream elements or concentrate on a particular scene in the dream. You'll read off evident implications of the surface of the dream, or bring psychoanalytic ideas to bear on the dream contents—oh, that dream of carnage was an oral aggressive dream, wasn't it?; or, I think there was an incestuous element in that dream of sexual contact with my sister; or whatever. But the best way to proceed is to allow your mind to wander about, select one dream image after another, and answer this question: *What other story, incident, memory, or other kind of narrative tale does this dream element bring to mind?* Varied narrative responses to this question make for rich encoded/thematic networks.

Think of each image in a dream as a story launcher; allow each image to evoke a free play of responsive stories. Each associated story should, as a rule, take you out of the scene of the manifest dream into some other scene. The various dream elements should move you out to as wide a variety of times, places, and persons as possible: a memory from childhood, a family incident from a few years ago, something from work but then something from a movie you've seen. Keep your memory and imagination loose. Memories from early childhood are especially valuable because they often reveal the roots of a current indicator, deepening your insight.

Just as the origination narrative is a response to an emotional trigger situation, free associations are similarly driven. As a rule they embody a variety of unconscious, encoded reactions to the trigger event: unconscious perceptions of its implications and meanings; connections between the trigger event and experiences from early childhood; a disguised picture of other responses that the trigger has evoked in you—aggressive, sexual, anxious, self-protective, vengeful, and the like; and camouflaged solutions to the conflicts the trigger has aroused.

Though your associations are concentrated on developing narrative content, remember that you are who you are, your defenses are there as they must be. Keep the process sufficiently open to allow for resistances because they are inevitable and for creative leaps because they are part of your unconscious gifts. Allow your mind to go where it wishes and watch where it takes you. Even as you structure and organize the self-analytic work, you must be open to the unexpected, a departure from the task at hand, and whatever else might come along. You walk a fine line between the Scylla of too narrow a confinement to each systematic step of the process and the Charybdis of too loose a sequence with too much randomness. Vigilance helps keep a proper balance.

oooo

Al is a physician in his mid-forties, an internist who is married to Laurel, his second wife. One morning he remembers a dream:

> He is at a summer, sleep-away camp as camp doctor. He is watching two boys quarrel; they may be his sons. He's not sure if he should break up the fight, which has turned into a rough, potentially injurious wrestling match.

Al has a few minutes of free time and decides to analyze his dream. The idea of being a camp doctor is appealing; he had done that one summer and had enjoyed it. Clearly, his dream fulfills a wish to be out of the city and away at camp where all is peaceful and serene—Freud is right after all, dreams are the fulfillment of wishes, he thinks. The fight seems harmless enough—boys will be boys. But the dream seems mainly to be a reaction to the recent pressures in Al's practice; being a camp doctor would be an ideal way to get away from it all for a while.

After enjoying some idyllic images of camp life, Al hesitates: Is the part about the two boys quarreling trying to tell him that camp isn't a perfect escape after all? Or does it reflect something childish in himself—isn't he one or both of the boys? Is he involved in some kind of struggle, a conflict? Is he angry at someone? Could it be one of his colleagues? Well, actually he is annoyed at several of them these days. Or are the boys simply his two sons? They're nine and seven, and they have been wrestling a lot lately. Or could the physical contact have some latent homosexual meaning? Al's been in psychoanalysis and knows about these things. Is that his sons' unconscious issue; is it his?

Intrigued by his own speculations—conscious system analyses are quite seductive—Al decides to look more carefully at the dream. He has an image now—an addendum—of a man off to the side in the door to one of the bunks; he too is watching the boys wrestle. Could that be Al's father? His father used to enjoy watching Al and his brother wrestle in the backyard of their home. Was that why Al didn't know whether to stop the fight or let it go on? Was he behaving like his father in allowing it to continue?

You might argue that there are other ways that Al could have looked directly at this dream and come away with more important meanings. That's a common debate among both amateur and professional conscious system psychotherapists: Whose interpretation of a dream is correct? But without clear guidelines as to what is and is not really meaningful, anybody's guess is as good as anyone else's. The same arbitrariness applies to this kind of seeming self-analysis: It all sounds good, makes sense, has a point—but it's actually relatively inconsequential conscious system material (though who can prove that point either?). There are no winners, only losers.

My point for the moment is that dreams are not dreamed to be studied at face value, they are dreamed to be associated to and decoded. The question to ask of a remembered dream is *not* something like: Why did I dream that?; What could it mean?; Who are those two boys?; Why summer camp?; What else can I remember from this dream?; What part of me do the boys represent?; What is my dream wish, my unconscious fantasy? Don't question a dream; don't formulate its meanings; don't ask for more dream images; don't speculate about what the dream or its cast of characters could represent. In other words, don't confront, analyze, or press a manifest dream—associate to it.

And even though I've described the nature of ideal free associations, you may well be wondering if I'm not being hypercritical of what Al came up with. After all, he did think about the dream; weren't those his associations to his dream? But while anything that comes to mind when thinking about a dream can be considered associations to that dream, some associations lead us to the deep wisdom within ourselves and others lead us away from that knowledge. Associations that take you into contexts that are different from those of the manifest dream are not taking you off the path to discovering encoded meaning—shifting contexts *is* the path to deep insight.

Anne is in her twenties. One morning she remembers this dream:

> She is on a subway platform and a man is tearing her purse from her hands and running away.

Looking this dream in the eye tells us that Anne is feeling vulnerable, abused by a man or men who run away from her. A rose is a rose is a rose; a dream of being attacked is feeling attacked is feeling vulnerable is every woman's—and man's—story on some level; there are no surprises and nothing specific to Anne and her personal life. And no matter how much more you would add to these formulations, they would still be in the same limited class.

So what then does free-associating add to this mix? To the subway, Anne associates an incident in which a man actually tried to take her briefcase from her; she is an attorney and the consequences for herself and her client would have been disastrous had he succeeded. She also recalls riding the subway with her father as a child; once when he was with her, a man exposed himself to her.

To the purse, Anne associates money and a raise she had gotten recently through the help of her division head. He's independently wealthy and has been making seductive overtures toward her. Running reminds Anne of a time that she was in a park and heard footsteps behind her; convinced it was a man who was going to try to assault or rape her, she had run away. The other night she had seen a movie in which a woman was raped and yet was held accountable for the incident. She recalls a novel about a woman who becomes involved with a man with whom she works, only to find herself nearly murdered when the affair turns sour and she threatens to tell the man's wife about it.

These are all rich stories, powerful associations to the dream elements, images that organize around themes of men doing harm and violence, sexual and otherwise, to women. This is a dream/associational network with strongly coalescing themes. It's the kind of network that is likely to be fraught with encoded meaning and apt to produce a memorable piece of self-analysis.

In this instance, it was not Anne's seductive supervisor who was creating the most disturbing triggers for this mass of themes, but sexual overtures from the husband of her best friend. When this trigger registered, it was relatively easy for Anne to organize these associations and their themes into a cogent view of a specific emotional issue in her life whose nature would elude her were she to confine her thoughts to the manifest dream alone.

Associated stories should jump about and involve one un-related thing after another. This shifting panorama is the sign of an especially rich associational network. The more diverse and full your bag of stories, the more you will learn from your deep wisdom system as you analyze and synthesize your dream.

There is, however, a problem. As you might expect, no matter how motivated and sensitive you are, and no matter how open to unconscious expressions you wish to be, at times the alliance between your deep fear/guilt system and your conscious system will, without your control, see to it that your associations are flat, intellectualized, and empty. While this is especially true when you are dealing with overwhelming triggers, extremes of trauma, it can also crop up because of unconscious sensitivities, incidents to which you are especially vulnerable. None of us can sustain ideal associations for very long; we always cycle away from encoded meaning, for resistances and unproductive moments crop up. But these too, having had their turn, cycle away in time; this is part of why we should do self-analysis on a daily basis—so we can catch the ripe and meaningful moments and help the empty efforts to pass on as quickly as possible.

Let's go back to Al. Knowledgeable in trigger decoding, he soon gets down to some serious free-associating. The questions he asks himself are these: What does each of these dream images bring to mind?; Where does each of these dream elements send me?; What else do I think of when I think of this dream?

The two boys, whom Al had pretty much ignored in his conscious ruminations, now attract his musings. He thinks of a film he had seen in which two sisters were bitter enemies; one of them has a secret affair with the other's husband. My wife has a sister and they are often at odds, he thinks. Her sister has been involved with a married man, her neighbor, but then again, this is what my first wife had done—which was why I divorced her.

This is a good start—clear and specific associated stories with well-defined themes. And we can see already that while the manifest dream content is mostly pleasant, the associational network is mostly unpleasant; each is centered on its own, distinct set of themes, and the manifest contents of the dream in this case do not hint at the associated material in any way.

Al goes back to associating. A few years ago one of his colleagues actually took a vacation from his practice and spent two months as a camp doctor. His wife had an affair with the camp director who lived in the cabin next to theirs—he was their neighbor, Al notices—and they too had ended up divorced.

Affairs with neighbors are at the center of his associations to the dream. He has at least one set of themes that must reflect his unconscious perceptions and their meanings; but to complete the picture, he needs the triggers that are evoking them. At that moment the incident that would be obvious to the rest of us hits Al: Last night, the night of the dream, he and his wife had entertained three couples for dinner, two of them neighbors. And somehow, Al had been very annoyed with his wife, Laurel. He had begun to wonder if he belonged in their marriage, yet he had no idea what had set off his doubts. Unexplained feelings of this kind are to be taken as indicators of the need for self-analysis.

Al finally remembers being disturbed by his wife's playing up to one of their male neighbors. And now that he thinks about it, this impression is supported by an odd, out-of-context story Laurel had told at dinner; it concerned two couples, neighbors, who had created a wild and un-manageable ménage à quatre. It took little time for Al to identify the suspected meanings of this encoded anecdote; his unconscious receptors must have picked up the implied meanings in this tale, even though he had not given it a second thought at the time Laurel had told it. Nor had Al consciously recognized that his wife was being flirtatious. Only when he associated to his dream, identified the main themes in his associational network, and used these themes to lead him to his triggers did Al understand the uncon-scious basis for his doubts about his marriage. Without trigger decoding, he might well have been headed unwit-tingly toward a second divorce; with decoding, he could identify and discuss the underlying issues directly with his wife and possibly resolve them. What we are not aware of we cannot negotiate.

This idyllic dream surface, with only a hint of struggle, involves an entirely different set of issues from the latent, unconscious concerns. Where the direct examination of this dream involved Al's sons and his father, the associative examination involved his wife and their neighbor. Associ-ations are the key to discovery.

At this point, Al still lacks some kind of validation of his new impressions. He turns to the shadowy figure who had reminded him of his father. Now that he is in the free-association mode, he thinks of a novel he is reading in which a man follows—shadows—his wife only to discover that she is having an affair with his closest friend.

Al can take the emergence, in an encoded story, of themes that support his decoded insight as confirmation that he is on the right track. A series of validating images would place his viewpoint on even more solid ground; you must be prepared to confirm your decoded formulations again and again in the course of self-analysis.

All associations are *not* equal; they can be graded for the extent to which they facilitate the self-analytic process.

Grade 1 associations are stories of *specific incidents* with a beginning, middle, and end. Often you'll find yourself distracted away from the full associative narrative; the end of the story often contains an important punch line—don't miss it.

Grade 1 associative stories must move away from the time, place, and people of the manifest dream into a new locale with new players—the more remote from the dream setting, the better. Relax when you free-associate; try not to force a story. Let the stories come to you with as little pursuit as possible. Fill in as much of the story line as you can. And never settle for just one story—there's usually two or more to be had. The more associated stories, dream elements, and themes you evoke, the greater the opportunity for discovering repetitive themes and the stronger the likelihood of successful self-analysis that ends with a fresh piece of decoded insight.

Grade 2 associations are also stories, but they are closer to the origination story than grade 1 associations. For example, the setting may remain the same in both narratives, or some or all of the people who populate both may be identical, but these are new stories, not merely another version of the manifest dreams. Also included in this category are broad narratives, such as generalizations about one's childhood ("We were poor when I was young"), a summary of the plot of a movie ("It was about a man and woman who have an affair"), or a global description of an incident ("We were in a bad car accident"). General narratives of this kind should lead to more specific recountings.

Al's association to his sons' quarreling is a grade 2 association: His sons are involved in both the manifest dream and this association, yet the theme of siblings in conflict emerges from the associations more clearly than in the dream.

Don dreams of a jewelry store. His association is to a store he frequents, and he recalls a recent robbery there. This is a grade 2 association; the store is common to both the dream and the association, but the association introduces a nonmanifest theme—that of a criminal act.

Grade 3 associations are the weakest kind of associated stories; they repeat the themes in a dream and add little new thematic content. Al's associations to being at camp—his liking the setting, enjoying his work as a camp doctor one summer, and his thoughts about his son's wrestling appear much as they had in the dream/associational network.

Edna dreams of a cut on her arm. She associates to a recent leg injury. This is a grade 3 association in that there is some degree of change from dream to association, but it is minimal. Grade 3 associations are very common when loss is the evocative trigger.

Grade 4 associations lack narrative qualities. Conscious efforts to identify the themes in the manifest dream material and to think about the people and places and action in the dream are grade 4 associations. Speculating that someone in a dream stands for someone else is a grade 4 association; though there is a representation, there is no story line and therefore the association receives a low rating.

At times, playing with these images on their own terms

will lead you to a story, so there's a whisper of a hope with this type of speculating. But most often, once you enter the conscious system mode, you'll stay in it and not shift to the narrative mode for a long while.

Dennis creates a short story in which a man attacks and stabs a woman in the park. He associates by recognizing that the story contains themes of violence, directed especially toward women. This is merely a summary of the manifest contents of the dream, not a fresh narrative. Yet thinking about these themes might eventually bring Dennis to both his dream trigger (a violent quarrel with his mother) and to more elaborate narrative associations (to a novel he'd just read about a young man who murders his grandmother over money).

It is advisable to use conscious vigilance to fight against all forms of intellectualizing as best you can; at the very least, when you get into this kind of rut, shift to self-observation; recognize your resistances. Then you can try to associate to that realization in the hope of discovering the source of the obstacle. It may well be that you're approaching a particularly disturbing area of association or insight.

Grade 5 associations include all efforts to interpret, understand, diagnose, prophesize, read into, formulate, list out, and otherwise deal directly with a manifest dream. These intellectualizations deceive us into thinking we've come up with answers to the meanings of our dreams, but they almost never provide answers to our indicators and triggers; they speak for resistance rather than insight.

High-quality free-associating typically generates surprising and intriguing stories whose revelations resonate deeply. Encoded communication has a kind of harmonic structure that flat intellectualizations lack. One of the most important ways to develop your own self-observational capacities is by sensing and experiencing the difference between stale ruminations and richly evocative narrative associations.

We build a dream/associational network so that we can use it for self-analysis. The main role of such a network is to present us with themes that are traceable to the deep unconscious wisdom system. Themes give us one-half of what we need; triggers provide the other half—themes are responses to triggers. We extract themes from narratives, so appreciating thematic content is the next step in self-analysis.

8 · Extracting Themes

NO MATTER HOW serious the underlying issues, trigger decoding should have a playful quality. The most essential part of the game involves *themes and triggers*: extracting the significant themes from our narrative/associational complex, and identifying and understanding the implications of the triggers that provoke our emotional responses. These two efforts are at the heart of self-analysis.

Triggers beget themes; themes reflect triggers and their unconscious meanings. Together, they hold the secret to our emotional lives and issues; they reveal the unconscious structure of our indicators. Separated, one kept from the other, these two elements tell us very little. Shorn of its specific trigger, a theme is an isolated image—a concern, dynamic thread, or issue that is easily subjected to rumination and speculation.

You look at a dream/associational network, for example, and observe that you are concerned about your mother or father, or abandonment, or sexuality, or aggression, or death. Often you will fail to notice that the same issues hold for everyone, that these are the ever-present problems of life. Our search is for something more specific and commanding.

There are two ways in which to engage in self-processing properly: You can go from recalling an origination narrative to free-associating, and then move directly to listing your triggers—leaving the job of extracting themes for last; or you can go from a focal narrative to associating and then directly to extracting themes before you deal with your trigger experiences. In general, the looseness of self-analysis allows for a mixture of both sequences, though the second method is usually more effective. Throughout the process, the goal is eventually to defeat our major communicative defense: keeping triggers separated from the themes to which they are unconsciously linked.

How do we identify the thematic contents of our narratives, and by what means do we extract all of the relevant meanings and implications we need for the decoding process? Recall that the dreams, daydreams, and stories we create are narratives with images and meaning—thematic content. *Themes are the linking element between a raw unconscious perception of a particular implication of a trigger situation on the one hand and an encoded conscious image on the other hand.* The deep unconscious wisdom system uses displaced themes to communicate with the outer world—our conscious minds. We experience a trigger situation, process its meanings and implications consciously and unconsciously, and the unconscious part of our reaction is relocated into a story about something other than the immediate trigger experience. The disturbing meanings of the stressful trigger situation are preserved and simply transported from the original issue into another setting. The process of disguise allows an anxiety-provoking unconscious experience to remain outside of awareness, even though it now finds camouflaged expression.

To understand how we develop our themes, a brief review of the sequence that leads to theme formation will be of help. The deep wisdom system perceives subliminally everything that is too disturbing for conscious experience. This deep system detects an implication or meaning in what has been unconsciously perceived, works over the constellation of raw perceptions and recognized meanings, and now wants to report on what it has fathomed and recommends as a response. It casts about for persons, places, and things that resemble its raw experiences and presents them in *disguised form*.

When we allow the deep unconscious wisdom system to speak out, it does so through one or another type of origination narrative and through narrative associations to these core stories. It is from this network of storied events, people, and action that we single out thematic contents: We catalog them, refine them, abstract their meanings, find common threads, and organize them into a meaningful whole. The image chosen for conscious expression—the encoded message—is always a narrative whose surface themes share important elements with the underlying unconscious image and themes.

As common psychoanalytic knowledge tells us, a room is a womb (both are enclosures), a telephone pole is a phallus (both are elongated), leaving on a train to go to a foreign place or crossing a river or larger body of water is death (journeys into the beyond or unknown); symbols share a common thread—a property—with whatever they symbolize. But these are universal symbols, at once personal and impersonal. Though we may gather such meanings as we search for themes, we must understand that they are of little import if they are not relocated into an active trigger situation.

There are also personal symbols, themes we might not otherwise identify without knowledge of an individual's personal investment in the image; this is a common form of thematic representation that often goes unnoticed. For example, a bus for Ed symbolizes love because he asked his wife to marry him on a bus. And likewise, for Ed a car is a symbol of harm because a good friend died recently in an accident. Each of us has many images with personal meanings; this is why the dreamer can generate the richest and most meaningful associations to his or her own origination narrative.

Finally, there are themes inherent to a particular image or event. While these themes tend to have a degree of universal consensus, they nonetheless have a personal element as well. A dream of being stabbed in the arm embodies themes of violence for everyone. Still, there are personal nuances: For one person, the act stresses violence; for another, bodily harm; for still another, the loss of blood. A variety of themes can be extracted from a given image; a good dream decoder can select those themes that are most pertinent to the issues raised by the trigger experience.

The deep unconscious wisdom system creates symbols in two ways. First, it can send a signal to the conscious system's memory bank that asks for a recollection with just the right amount of disguise; this can range from extremely well-camouflaged images to images that are only slightly altered. In the first instance, there is only a faint or very abstract connection between the raw perception and the encoded conscious vehicle—for example, the use of a tweezers to encode a clawing mother. In the second case, the connecting threads are clear and strong, as seen, for example, in the use of a witch with long fingernails to encode the same clawing mother figure. Whatever the encoded conveyance, some common thread must exist between the deep and surface messages.

The second means of producing a conscious narrative with encoded meanings—themes—involves our unique unconscious capacity to use our imagination, to create unprecedented images that serve the purpose of disguised expression. *The creative center* generates the unconscious part of our creativity; it is a part of the mind where any theme we need to express our unconscious reactions to triggers can be created out of nothing. The creative center can be extraordinarily inventive; you can dream or daydream of flying, possessing Herculean powers, having babies long past menopause or before puberty. All of these inventions encode unconscious responses to an emotional trigger.

There are four steps to theme analysis:

First, you identify the specific themes contained in your conscious narratives; many kinds and levels may be detected.

Second, you lift the theme out of its surface story and allow it to stand as an extracted or abstracted, isolated theme, no longer connected to its surface context.

Third, you restore the theme back into its original context, which is the trigger situation; that is, you identify the evocative trigger for the created theme and link the theme to the trigger.

And fourth, you use the relocated theme to understand your unconscious reaction to the trigger experience; the freshly created theme-trigger link gives new meaning to the trigger event.

The entire process is silently directed by your sense of

the implications of the active triggers, which serves as an unobtrusive guide in selecting the thematic meanings that you will use.

Themes can be extracted from narrative material at three levels:

1. *Concrete themes.* These are the concrete images of a narrative, essentially unmodified. Jed dreams of a tall, muscular man lifting him high into the air. The themes are tallness, muscularity, lifting, being up high, and being in the air; no implications or addenda are invoked. Themes as themes are a good level on which to start a mental list.

2. *Specific abstractions and implications.* On this level, you take some liberties and accept the inevitable risk of distortion or error. You look at a theme in its manifest context and extract some evident implications that are not directly stated in the narrative itself. On this level, Jed's dream suggests themes of stature (tallness), strength (muscular and lifting), and being in the upper stratosphere (high in the air).

Use caution when listing implications mentally, though as you are the dreamer of the dream and the creator of the associations to it, you should give serious consideration to your own sense of the implications of an image. The implications that others propose are open to considerable distortion and projection; rarely can others accurately appraise a meaning you intended to convey and missed. Nonetheless, outsiders may pick up an implication of an image that you, as dreamer, had a defensive need to bypass. As a rule, it is advisable to determine if any implication someone else suggests in response to your narrative reverberates with your own associations and extends them into additional thematic threads. If the proposed themes lead to fresh material that also works well with your triggers in explaining your indicators, then a positive contribution has been made.

3. *General, symbolic, and highly abstract implications.* This level of theme extraction is continuous with level 2, but at a higher level of abstraction—there is a greater distance between the concrete image and the extracted theme. This level also includes more remote or uncertain implications, allowing for some looseness when you propose themes suggested by narrative/associational images. The symbolic implications of an image belong on this level. For Jed's dream, level 3 implications could include physical contact with a man and, even more remotely, suggestions of latent homosexuality; masculine strength and power, or strength and power per se; rising up, reaching higher goals; and passive submission to the power of others.

Your goal in general is to discover thematic threads on all three levels and to organize these threads into a fabric of collected meanings that needs only to be given a pattern by one or more organizing triggers.

Edith is preoccupied with a newspaper story of a woman whose cat miraculously survived a fall from a sixth-story window. The concrete, level 1, themes include a newspaper, woman, cat, miracle, survival, fall, sixth story, and window. Level 2 implications are public information and reporting (the newspaper); felines, animals (the cat); the unexpected and the unusual, a remarkable occurrence (the miraculous quality); overcoming likely death and bodily harm (survival); and falling from an opening (the sixth-story window).

Level 3 implications might include exposure and spreading the word (newspaper); women and their possessions (woman with cat); being catty (the cat); magic and the unbelievable (miracle); defeating death, attack, or other adversity (surviving); loss of control and falling; being unprotected and improperly cared for, and dangerous openings (going out the window).

With themes, there's always more, but if you capture the main elements, you will have more than enough to work with. For Jed, the trigger involved a series of moves by his boss to improve his position in his firm; the anxiety he felt while being held on high was primarily his fear of success. For Edith, the trigger was a pending hysterectomy. You can see how the themes organize around each of these triggers and how themes that appear to be unrelated and scattered actually come together and synthesize once the trigger is known.

We can look now at a more elaborate illustration of the search for themes. Leah has a daydream:

She is a part of a team of women scientists who invents a powerful ray that destroys cancer cells.

Leah is a graduate student in physics and thinks of her daydream as pure wish fulfillment. But she does proceed to identify her themes: concretely (level 1), there are themes of being part of a team, a team of women; women, scientists; invention and power; a ray, and destroying cancer cells. On level 2, there are implied themes such as group cooperation, women together, creativity and discovery, a penetrating beam, a curative form of destruction, and disease, physical illness. On level 3 she has produced implications regarding closeness between women; latent homosexual possibilities; the exclusion of men; science and research and exactness; a beam that seems, symbolically, to have phallic powers that are capable of destroying the destroyer; and cells that proliferate, infiltrate, devour, and destroy their host. We can sense from these themes alone that Leah is absorbed in some way in a mighty struggle with issues related to womanhood, creativity, penetration, illness, and cure.

Leah has an association to the curative ray: It involves a story reported on television of a new form of chemotherapy for lung cancer. The experimental drug was in short supply, and the report concerned a woman with lung cancer who could not get the drug and had filed a protest. However, the medical board of the hospital had ruled that she had been treated fairly in that the researchers had used a lottery to determine who would receive the medication.

This is a grade 1 association, rich in additional themes for Leah to identify; concretely, there is a television report, new cure, a form of chemical therapy, lung cancer, scarcity of the drug, woman unable to get the drug, filing a protest, hospital's medical board ruling that the woman was treated fairly, a lottery determining who receives the drug. Identifying concrete themes is a way of dividing the imagery into segments that can then be extracted, moved about by themselves, and eventually brought to rest within the framework of their triggers.

On level 2, Leah's associations seem to contain themes of exhibitionism and public exposure (television); a new form of therapy, chemical cure, curative drug, healer of cancer; cancer itself: illness, bodily destruction; research and uncertainty of the cure; an insufficiency of the drug that leads to being unable to help everyone and favoring some people over others; being deprived of the cure, not getting needed help; objecting, rebelling against the decision made; ruling body and judgment, fairness and chance (the lottery).

These themes are extended by such level 3 themes as voyeurism (television); a toxic substance that heals; being eaten up alive (cancer); an unfair situation in which matters of life and death are decided according to luck and chance; protesting against and being angry with those in control; and siding with the researchers against the patient.

In all likelihood, you yourself have thought of some themes Leah missed; you'd have to share them with Leah to find out if your associations are useful to her. You can see too that as the associations accumulate, themes multiply rapidly. But certain themes will repeat themselves, as they do here with Leah—for example, new cure, cancer, and cure via a process that is usually harmful. Be alert for these repetitive themes; they are especially meaningful. But you should also mentally mark all new themes that emerge with fresh associations.

Along about now, you may be asking: This seems so complicated, I'm going to miss a lot, why can't I write down these themes and work them over from there? This is a beguiling conscious system plea, but don't succumb to it. Self-analysis takes care of itself in a way; whatever you miss the first time around is sure to be recycled again and again until you catch it. And the essence of effective self-exploration directed toward bringing forth the truly unknown and otherwise unknowable is a free play of narratives, associations, themes, triggers, and indicators. This openness is especially critical for free-associating; interrupting the flow of self-processing in order to record dreams and themes radically disrupts the flow of associations and the back-and-forth movement between the various elements of the process. Have faith in yourself as a self-analyzer: You can do it well, just give yourself time to get used to it.

oooo

Leah's themes seem to organize around illness and cure—
first the cure is available, then there's someone (a woman)
who is deprived of the cure. At this juncture, Leah could
have been drawn into intellectualizing: She could argue that
she is concerned about illness in herself or someone else
(most probably a woman), and that she's either uncertain
about the cure or ambivalent about how it should turn out.
This is a selective and very broad summary of a few of
these themes. At best, this isolated set of themes might be
used to suggest possible triggers—for example, is Leah or
someone close to her ill? But broad sweeps of this kind,
detached from triggers, tend to be far more defensive than
revealing. It is better to stick to specifics—working with
particular themes in search of definitive triggers—than to
engage in this kind of triggerless guesswork.

To illustrate, Leah now remembers that she had learned
that very day that a woman member of the physics department had been hospitalized for a lymphoma, a cancer of
the lymphatic system. While Leah's daydream speaks
plainly of saving the woman's life and of combating the
helplessness of being afflicted with a life-threatening illness,
her associated images speak for the added possibility of
failing. As always, there is a connection between the trigger
and the themes; the most obvious connecting images are
called *bridging themes or images*—themes that belong to both
the manifest image and the latent issue, the hidden trigger
situation. Here the bridging themes are found in the allusions to cancer and its cure—or not being able to get the
cure. These appear in Leah's manifest daydream and in her
associations as well as in the underlying trigger situation.

Leah did indeed have very mixed feelings toward this
woman. She was a brilliant role model but also had made

things difficult for Leah on occasion. But there was a deeper issue—a repressed trigger situation: Leah's mother was suffering from a serious form of heart failure, and she was taking an experimental drug in an effort to prevent a serious deterioration in her condition. Here the bridging themes are illness (rather than cancer per se) and experimental drug (a striking shared theme or link). Leah's ambivalence toward her mother is quite evident; we might also speculate that her use of the cancer idiom reflects a violent and murderous side to Leah's feelings toward her. Indeed, once a trigger has been identified and connected to themes, it's important to study each theme to determine how much is perception (at times, Leah's mother had been violently angry with her daughter), how much is fantasy/wish, and how much involves correctives—advice as to how to deal with the trigger experience.

In Leah's situation, her unconscious guilt over her violent perceptions of, and feelings toward, her mother had led to several self-destructive actions on her part, both in school and in her relationship with her boyfriend. Self-analysis of this network of themes and triggers helped her to move toward working her way out of these difficulties and to reduce her ambivalence toward her mother and mentor. Much of this came about because Leah's self-analytic work brought out perceptions and feelings of which she had been unaware—hidden issues that she could deal with and resolve now that they were out in the open.

This work with themes brings us at long last to the events and experiences that empower the entire network of narratives and associations and call forth our decoding efforts: the trigger experiences themselves. The search for triggers is the last part of the sequence of self-analysis before the final synthesis.

9 ° The Search for Triggers

ON THE FACE of it, the search for emotional triggers would seem to be the easiest part of self-analysis. You would think that all you needed to do after free-associating to a narrative is to go over in your mind the main emotional issues, decisions, and trauma you've had on your plate. But nothing in self-analysis comes that easily; there's always work to be done to overcome resistances.

I have been teaching self-analysis to small groups for some years now. Whenever an individual or group engages in a trigger listing exercise, there is a consistent pattern. The list begins with the most innocuous emotional issues at hand and almost reluctantly moves to more serious concerns. One or two of the most compelling triggers regularly slip through the cracks unless someone happens to pick them up as an afterthought. We instinctively avoid anxiety-provoking territories; we need to be powerfully motivated and robust to run counter to this trend.

Much the same defensiveness comes into play when you

attempt to identify the implications of an acknowledged trigger experience. You'll be inclined to think first of the meanings that are easy to handle, or the issues you've already resolved. Only with a great deal of effort and determination will you get to the distressing meanings that tend to cluster around sexuality, violence and aggression, sources of guilt, and death anxiety—and your own personal sensitivities.

These troublesome aspects of living are not general concerns but arise at particular moments and through definite incidents—they are specifically triggered. You can therefore be guided in your search for anxiety-provoking meanings by invoking self-observation and checking out these often-overlooked domains to see if anything recently has stirred up problems in these areas. From there, particular triggers may activate other life concerns, such as bodily anxieties over illness and injury, identity and self-esteem, competition and success, freedom versus restraints, activity versus passivity.

Someone suddenly disappears from your life, and yet it takes an inordinate amount of time to realize it's a trigger. You then try to list the implications of the incident and you come up with abandonment, desertion, loss—all the obvious translations. You also easily link the incident to the time in your childhood when your mother was hospitalized for pneumonia for six weeks, and to another time when your dog was hit by a car and died. Only later, after you've had a very violent and sexually sadistic dream and a few gruesome associations, do you begin to work over the fact that this was your lover who left you in an abrupt and insulting way and that you feel demeaned as a sexual partner, sexually assaulted, damaged bodily, and devastated. And with a little more effort, you also realize that you're so furious you could kill.

Though it's disturbing, you now have moved beyond your self-protective clichés to a real sense of how you react unconsciously to hurt and abandonment. You are then able to alert yourself to the inevitability that many of your subsequent actions—or symptoms—will be motivated by this violence constellation of perceptions and reactions. With this decoded wisdom in hand you can prevent disastrous forms of rationalized but hurtful behaviors that would cause suffering for yourself and others in the end. Insight of this kind allows for a conscious working over of the underlying issues so that emotional symptoms such as anxiety or phobias do not ensue.

Powerful conscious implications of triggers integrate with unconscious meanings, and it's never a pretty picture. Our first line of defense against this constellation lies in putting a trigger experience out of our minds. The backup protection is to minimize its conscious implications, while the deeper defense is to relegate to unconscious perception all of the most troublesome aspects of the experience. Still feeling endangered, we then resist decoding the disguised images that convey these unconscious realizations. If we do give it a try, we tend to avoid trigger decoding because it would finally bring into awareness the very meanings whose impact we are determined to keep in oblivion. If our lives were not governed by these unconscious meanings, we could let it all rest and go about our business. But unconscious meanings do empower our emotional lives, so there's work to be done after all.

The goal of self-analysis is to overcome the costly ways our minds naturally protect our survival mechanisms. Though the conscious mind believes it has struck a good bargain, careful scrutiny consistently shows that we actually pay dearly for this denial-based security. The cost in emotional pain to ourselves and others far exceeds the momentary relief we achieve.

As for the price side of this equation, we have already seen the hurtful decisions, conflicted relationships, emotional symptoms, and blindly destructive behaviors that come about when we operate without trigger-decoded wisdom. Think of everything in your life from which you are suffering, everything you'd like to change and can—but haven't. Think of the compromises you've made, the harm you've inadvertently caused yourself and others, and the conflicts you've gotten embroiled in, many of them still unresolved. And finally, think of idiosyncratic behaviors, such as eating too much, smoking, drinking, taking drugs, and bad habits you've never been able to give up. Add all of this up as a measure of the consequences of your ignorance of encoded wisdom. Look at the burdens created in the same way by family, friends, social community, country, and the world at large; small wonder we don't live in a peaceful world.

With trigger decoding, an enormous amount of this suffering and pain can be changed for the better. The process certainly will not solve all individual and collective emotional problems, but it can be more constructive than anything we've got going without it.

There are two main approaches to listing triggers and ascertaining their implications. The first is a *trigger sweep*, an attempt consciously to locate and list all of your known and active triggers—beginning with those of the current day, then moving to those of the previous day, and from there to triggers of relatively recent origin, and finally to those of earlier origin that still linger about unresolved. As a rule, we react first and foremost to very recent and immediately active triggers, though our minds are so structured that current traumas will always arouse memories of earlier, related incidents. If you haven't identified one or more significant immediate triggers, your list is incomplete and you must continue the search for these missing emotional stimuli. Self-analysis always begins in the present.

The second guide to discovering your triggers involves the themes from your narrative/associational network, *the themes-to-triggers approach*. To use it, you create your origination dream or other narrative, allow full time for free-associating, identify the prevailing themes, and allow the themes to suggest triggers. Triggers evoke themes, so themes are clues to triggers.

You are likely to have two kinds of experiences in taking this approach to your triggers: In the first, the themes-to-triggers connections are easily recognized, while in the second, the connections are less evident and more subtle. In the first instance, themes of money, for example, speak for financial triggers; themes of sexuality speak for sexual issues; and of loss speak for loss-related trigger events.

Despite the existence of relatively apparent links, you'll probably still find it easy to miss a critical trigger or two. After all, you are dealing with *emotionally charged recall*—you are reaching back to identify traumas that you wish to avoid. There is an unceasing struggle between the conscious system's natural wish to obliterate and forget and this new conscious motivation that you're developing to have memory and vision. As you become more familiar with your own sensitivities and defenses, you'll find it easier to fill in your blind spots and to carry forward the work of self-analysis. You can learn to beat the odds.

Once you've identified a trigger, spend some time dwelling on its apparent meanings. Struggle against the inclination to treat triggers as general issues; deal with them as specific problems that arise at a specific moment in your life, in the context of specific relationships. Your cousin's death does not mean that you are dealing with loss but is a specific way of losing someone whose interaction with you has had some particular meanings and created identifiable issues—gratifying and frustrating. Your demotion at work is not merely a demeaning and hurtful experience but a definite moment in your life in which the exact nature of the demotion, the job and relationship contexts, defines a specific trigger constellation.

Critical triggers often come to mind unexpectedly and draw you back to your thematic network in ways that you hadn't seen before. Triggers empower themes and place your unconscious stirrings meaningfully into the flow of your daily life. As humans, we tend to react to immediate stimuli; the longer the time between the trigger incident and the moment of self-analysis, the less power the trigger possesses to evoke unconscious reactions—though extremely traumatic triggers do tend to disturb the mental system so greatly that their effects can linger over a lifetime. This is why the self-analysis of an out-of-context or marginally related story told in the heat of an emotional exchange tends to produce such a highly decodable network of themes—the trigger is active at the very moment you have composed the narrative. With dreams and daydreams, there is some delay between the emotional moment and the instant at which the responsive story is remembered and associated to.

Triggers come in groups; life is complex and difficult emotionally. Even when a major trauma might well dominate the picture, other emotional issues lurk about in need of analysis. Persevere in your search for triggers until all trails have been exhausted.

During self-exploration, you will tend to move back and forth between themes and triggers, and among current and more distant but active trigger situations. Once you have established your initial narrative/associational network and themes, you should select a particular trigger experience and examine its conscious implications. In principle, you should analyze one trigger at a time. Try to extend your understanding of each trigger experience by turning to the narrative themes to develop your unconscious view of the issues it has stirred up. Often, working over a particular trigger to the point of decoded insight leads to fresh associations and thematic material. And while this may then lead to still another trigger and perhaps more fresh associations, the process will also tend to trail off once you have realized and put to use a solid insight from the deep unconscious wisdom system.

Nina is in her late forties, married with a daughter, Dehlia, who is twenty-five. Nina has been feeling depressed for the past two weeks, but she's unable to locate the source. Loyal to her husband, Phil, all these years, she's become uncharacteristically interested in a man at work, Curt, who has been making overtures toward her. She's puzzled by her attraction to him and struggling to keep from getting involved. She's also been annoyed with Phil and provocative toward him in ways that seem unreasonable. In addition, she's been eating more than usual and putting on weight.

Here again we see a slice of life: a series of indicators or emotional issues that seems inexplicable. As is true with triggers, indicators seldom come in single doses. And often they seem unrelated—a measure of anxiety here, an impulsive action there, an unnecessary interpersonal conflict as well—until the unconscious links are found.

In Nina's case, however, there seem to be some connecting threads between her various emotional symptoms: Overeating is often connected to depression and discontentment, while the attraction to Curt and her irritation with Phil also seem linked. Still, the deeper connections are hard to discern without using a trigger/theme complex to understand the unconscious sources and meanings of these signs of emotional disequilibrium.

What is setting me off? Nina wonders. Her conscious appraisal—for the moment isolated from any narrative material—is sparse, as it often is without a buildup of thematic contents. Lately her husband has been more aloof than usual; could she be feeling abandoned and turning to Curt as a substitute? Invoking self-vigilance, she realizes that all of this is too flat and self-evident to be of much use, so she continues to explore.

She thinks of her daughter who has left the nest, but Nina is pleased that Dehlia is finally on her own. She misses her daughter but feels that she has worked through her feelings of loss. Nina feels liberated and able to look forward to being free of the burdens of motherhood. Besides, Nina's brother lives in the city where Dehlia is working, so Nina expects to visit her soon. Reflecting back on her thoughts so far, Nina feels that nothing seems to explain her indicators.

That night, before falling asleep, she tries to remember her dreams of the previous night. Nothing comes to mind, and she feels stymied. Eventually she decides to invent a brief story:

There is a young woman traveling through Europe by herself. It feels like a grand holiday. She arrives by boat on a Greek island. She finds an isolated beach, disrobes, and glories in the radiance of the sun and sand.

Nina is unable to extend the story—she keeps picturing the woman, who is in her forties, lying on the beach. Not much of a story, she notes to herself, but it feels good—I'd sure like to be there myself. (The story is very much like a wish-fulfilling daydream; often these late-night inventions are far more grim and unpleasant than Nina's little tale— we tend to fail to remember our dreams when we are over-stressed and overburdened.) The woman is probably me, she concludes, stating the obvious.

Moving on, Nina notices that the themes in this story involve a woman, travel, Europe, being alone, holiday, boat, Greece, island, beach, nakedness, sun, and sand. Possible implications that occur to her involve both independence and aloneness, adventure, celebration, being isolated, and enjoying nature. The themes on all levels here are not very rich. While it's nice to be able to conjure up such images, it's well to recall that the stories created by the deep un-conscious wisdom system encode reactions to disturbing emotional triggers; we can seldom rest content on the soft sands of a blissful daydream. We need to dig deeper, and we do that not by trying to force the analysis further through direct confrontation with the images—it is clichéd to say that the woman must represent Nina or that this is a story of the pleasures of being on one's own— but by associating freely and openly to the origination nar-rative.

Nina does just that: She asks herself where the various images take her—to what other time, place, and person-ages; to what other stories? Her first thought is of a trip to a Caribbean island that she had made with Phil and Dehlia a year earlier. Dehlia had done some nude swimming and had told her parents a distressing tale of a married man who had become seductive with her, and whom she had repulsed. He didn't understand the rules of the beach, she had moaned, nude bathing is for freedom and liberation, it's not sexual—and especially not with a married man. Besides, he exposed himself in a way that made it all seem so obscene; some people just can't appreciate nature for what it is.

Nina had spent time with Dehlia on the beach. Like two children, they had built castles with the sand, only to see the waters wash them away. A woman had gone snorkeling and had been rescued from the menacing waters—a storm had been brewing—after she hit her head on a reef that rose up close to the surface. The storm had turned nasty and became a hurricane before it ended. From their room, Nina and Phil had watched the trees bend in the fierce winds. Later, in exploring the island, they discovered that some of the trees had been uprooted.

Associations continue to come to her mind. With a shift in time and place characteristic of strong grade 1 associations, Nina recalls that as a teenager, she had a fear of diving into the high school swimming pool. She remembers to this day the story of a young girl who was killed when she hit her head on the pool bottom because she mistakenly dove into shallow water. Shifting again, Nina recalls a story in the newspaper about a woman who sailed to some Pacific island by herself and who was marooned in a storm but eventually rescued.

Surrounded by riches of themes, Nina pauses to harvest the results of her associative efforts. There are many themes now; a dream of being alone in splendid isolation has been transformed into an associational network filled with people, danger, and reparation. Some of the initial themes are: island, family together, nudity and swimming, seductive married man, his exposing himself, repulsing him, obscenity, not understanding rules and when situations are non-sexual. Nudity has appeared again—it was in the original narrative—but now there are allusions to rules, married men, obscenity, and inappropriate seduction. These unexpected themes must in some way be clues to the important triggers that have stimulated this narrative/associational complex. The same triggers undoubtedly have also stirred up Nina's emotional indicators, and properly trigger-decoded, this network could well reveal their unconscious meanings. But Nina has some more work to do before integrating these separate pieces.

Nina thinks for a moment of Curt, but her mind pulls her away from him and returns to cataloging her themes. She picks up on the images (themes) of castles in the sand and their being washed away; and of snorkeling—looking—and being injured and then rescued. Bodily harm emerges as a theme and finds its echo in the later image of the girl who was killed diving into the swimming pool. Other themes that Nina marks involve watching the storm, trees that stand up against the winds, and other trees that are uprooted—a possible symbolic allusion again to both surviving and dying. There is also a repetition of the theme of being a woman alone, though now it is connected with being marooned by a storm and then rescued.

This pleasant origination narrative has spawned a very full and promising narrative/associational network. From the themes alone, Nina can tentatively formulate certain issues that she can then use in helping her to identify the missing triggers. There are salient themes of nudity and exposure, of impermanence and destruction, of fear of water and being submerged and of injury, and themes of reparation. There are references to independence that is glorious in one story and endangering in another (the contradiction suggests opposing views and needs). And there is the theme of inappropriate seduction, with refutation.

Nina has a sense of some prominent issues, but she realizes that to move ahead, it's time to start listing her triggers so she can better fathom these themes. She thinks immediately of a call she had received from her daughter earlier that evening. While it was never explicitly stated, and though she hadn't noticed it at the time, there was an air of distress and desperation in what Dehlia had said. The job she had taken wasn't working out as hoped, and the salary had turned out to be less than promised. Had Dehlia been calling for help? If so, Nina had missed it at the time, partly because Dehlia had quickly covered over her concerns with positive thoughts and allusions to promises made for future changes that would make the situation more satisfying.

Nina was now able to use this particular trigger to organize the thematic material into a set of unconscious perceptions that had eluded her conscious thinking about her daughter. Dehlia had been seduced into moving by the head of the company for which she was now working. She had indicated earlier to Nina that her boss was a smooth talker, attractive but married, and that he had filled her with alluring promises; but she insisted that she could handle him and the job situation without difficulty. On a deeper level, Nina had sensed a strong physical attraction between her daughter and this man; this issue had also been hinted at in Dehlia's call, though it too had gone unnoticed until now.

Dehlia had talked at length about a woman at work who

had repulsed the advances of her married section chief. It seems certain in retrospect that Nina had unconsciously seen this tale for what it was: an encoded message for both of them. This story aroused comparable issues within Nina; she needed to get to them. But for the moment, her thought was that independence is, after all, both liberating and endangering.

Nina feels concern for the safety of her daughter. This leads her to a second trigger: That day at work, Curt had suggested that Nina stay late and put in some overtime on a project on which they were both working. Nina had planned to meet Phil after work for dinner, and she had thought of canceling but decided not to do it. Laughingly, she said she'd take a rain check on the offer from Curt and then added that maybe they could have a drink together instead of always being bottled up at work. Surprised by the words that came tumbling out of her mouth—a sign of a compelling indicator—Nina immediately withdrew the offer.

Here Nina could make good use of the themes and the ideas developed around the first trigger involving her daughter to flesh out a series of unconscious perceptions related to the situation with Curt. She now extracts her themes and insights from the conversation with Dehlia and relates them to her conversation with Curt. She can see that unconsciously, she saw Curt as inappropriately seductive; he too is a married man. But she herself had been inadvertently seductive; both of them had inappropriately exposed their sexuality to each other. These themes encode an important perception of Nina's own actions that she had not fully appreciated at the time of the incident. In a way, neither she nor Curt understood the rules; and her deep unconscious wisdom system was cautioning her that she shouldn't mix business with pleasure, nor should married people have affairs.

Clearly, Nina's unconscious assessment of a situation she consciously found alluring—one that might rescue her from the damaging aspects of her marriage—was nonetheless focused on an encoded view that saw the involvement with Curt as distinctly dangerous. On one level, the outcome is portrayed as a disaster—a hurricane and death.

Perhaps the most compelling advice that her encoded wisdom system offered to her is disguised in her daughter's invocation of the need to follow rules and to keep certain situations as nonsexual; this admonition is reinforced in Dehlia's repudiation of the advances of the married man on the beach and her business associate's rejection of seductive advances from a married section chief.

These insights lead Nina to recall a woman friend who had had an affair with a coworker that had turned sour and led to her friend's suicide attempt. That was enough encoded confirmation of Nina's understanding to evoke a strong resolve to pull back from Curt.

While still more could be organized around this second trigger, Nina chooses to pursue other triggers that come to mind as she works over this vast territory of themes, emotional issues, and feelings. At dinner Phil had spoken in a tense and overinvolved way about a woman customer he was servicing, qualities that register only now as Nina extends her list of triggers. Do her two prior narrative/thematic networks encode an unconscious perception of Phil as being unfaithful to her? As these are speculations about someone else, and involve unconscious perceptions, Nina realizes that she must proceed with caution. Still, her sudden recall at this point of a story she saw in the TV news about a woman who murdered her husband when she found him in bed with another woman gives Nina more cause for concern. It's now all too easy to link these images to her recent depression, and her provocativeness and anger with Phil, and with her own thoughts of infidelity. When thematic networks begin to weave together like this, there is a considerable probability that the ideas involved are sound.

Without pursuing other thematic connections to her conversation with Phil—she returned to it later—Nina tries to think of still more triggers. There are some problems with her house, and repairmen have been engaged who don't do the jobs they promise to do. There's also been some conflict with May, Nina's closest friend, who wants to go away on vacation alone with Nina, while Nina would rather stay at home right now and prepare for her visit to Dehlia. These triggers seem more routine to Nina— examples of normal stress. Having slipped back a bit to lesser issues, Nina feels stymied; she decides to allow the themes in her images to suggest fresh triggers.

Some workmen had been in the house the day before and had left it in disarray. Unconsciously Nina had felt physically damaged; she was also angry with Phil because she had asked him not to allow the men into the house until she had cleared away some of the furniture they eventually damaged. This kind of vulnerability greatly bothered Nina; she had forgotten the incident until now. This seemingly minor disturbance also touched on earlier experiences—ways in which Nina's mother had failed to protect her from the barbs and physical attacks of her older brother and sister as a child.

Independence, travel, and surviving storms now bring forth another trigger that Nina had repressed. Her closest associate at work, Peggy, would be leaving the firm the next day. Peggy's husband, Ezra, had died ten months before, and she decided to leave her job and travel for a while before seeing where she wanted to go with her life. Now that Nina thinks of it, Ezra had died of a brain tumor. The images of the castles washed away by the ocean—the passing sands of time—and of nonfatal and fatal head injuries connect Nina's themes to the loss of both Peggy and her husband.

How nice, Nina thinks: Here I am dealing with the death of husbands and friends, and the loss of my daughter, and I tell myself a story of an idyllic Greek island beach. No wonder that lovely bit of denial didn't hold up too long. And can there be any question as to why I'm feeling depressed and angry with the world—and deprived as well? I can see now why I'm overeating myself to death; I'd better stop punishing myself that way. How wonderful it would have been if Ezra had been rescued—cured—but he wasn't. He was one of the trees that was uprooted, as Peggy is now and my daughter before her.

Only after much additional associating, analyzing, and synthesizing does Nina finally recover one last trigger—at which point she reaches the limit of what she can handle in one self-analytic session. Her brother's daughter, who is only nineteen, had developed a rare form of cancer of the thyroid gland. The gland had been surgically removed, and she was receiving chemotherapy; there is hope that she will survive without further spread or metastases. Yet there is also grave concern for her future.

In light of this trigger, the narrative/associational/insight network reorganizes in a way that stresses the images of physical damage and concern about death—will her niece survive the hurricane of her cancer or be uprooted and die? All of this brings forth many more ideas, but eventually takes Nina back to age five and a tonsillectomy she had undergone; a host of new images related to the dread of annihilation and issues of survival come up as well. Nina finally falls off to sleep, heavily loaded with serious concerns and realizations, but in possession of some likely solutions to her conscious and unconscious conflicts as a result of her self-exploration.

We can see why we so often want to stop the process before we get to the grim issues; but these are the issues that unconsciously run our lives. The affair that her husband might be having and the illness of her niece depressed Nina. This last caused her to feel a kind of survivor guilt that led to her overeating; and both triggers prompted her to consider an affair that was revealed as self-destructive in the long run. Her anger at Phil had many sources: There was his possible affair, and his being a man who is freer to roam the world and who is less vulnerable to thyroid cancer than women in general—and Nina in particular. And this anger also came in part because of still another unanalyzed trigger: Phil's sister was suffering from a malignancy that Nina didn't wish to deal with. Web enmeshed in web; such is the unconscious structure of our emotional lives.

So we see now the kinds of triggers that activate our deep unconscious system—wisdom and fear/guilt. To use the wisdom, play out your themes before taking on your triggers. Take nothing for granted except for defensiveness, however subtle, at every turn. And be wary of wanting to discard a recognized trigger from the unfolding self-analysis by invoking a generalization or dismissing the importance of an issue. Be sure to use the network drawn around one trigger as encoded meanings for the next trigger you happen upon. Don't hesitate to go back to a trigger you feel you've already understood in light of new stories and themes; there's always more to learn.

One final piece of advice: Keep it simple at first; work with just one trigger and just a couple of themes, and use the network to explain a single indicator. Given that bump you gave yourself on your head and the anxiety you're experiencing, it's enough to know that your husband's staying out until three in the morning had triggered that brief dream of a man's head split open and that quick association to a woman who hit her philandering husband over the head with a baseball bat. Though relatively simple in structure, this neat network tells you a great deal of your encoded perceptions of your husband's act and your unconscious wishes to have your revenge—which, through guilt, you evidently took out on yourself.

Themes and triggers; two sides of the same coin. Together they tell us more about ourselves and others, and about the emotional side of life, than any other known level or form of communication. But triggers must be understood in terms of themes, and themes understood in terms of triggers. For that, we need some rules of analyzing and synthesizing, which is next on our agenda.

10 ◦ Achieving Insight and Healing

WE COME NOW to the payoff for the entire self-analytic process: arriving at a moment of insight. We carry out self-analysis in order to solve an emotional problem or understand an emotional issue. We call the solution, the understanding we achieve, *insight*.

Hypothetically, there's true or genuine (emotional) insight, but there are intellectual and false insights as well. You'll find that almost everyone has a different definition of the first kind of understanding; it's easy to get lost in the maze of claims and counterclaims. Pseudoinsight takes many more forms than does the real thing. Your fear/guilt system typically drives your direct reading of a dream to wrong conclusions—like deciding to take off after a dream of leaving home because you believe your dream is telling you what to do.

For some people, including many psychotherapists, anything we didn't know before we initiated self-exploration passes as a form of insight. Psychoanalysts usually define insight as making conscious something that previously was unconscious. But just as we saw that many types of communication, ideas, and meanings exist beyond awareness, so too there are many ways in which something outside of awareness can become part of our conscious thinking. And while anything that expands our range of awareness is of some value, it is only those insights that derive from the encoded wisdom system that can really make a profound difference in our lives.

The deep wisdom insights we want are of two kinds: The first helps us to understand something that we did not previously comprehend; the second brings into awareness solutions to our emotional problems that are entirely unavailable through conscious deliberation. Recall that the deep unconscious wisdom system reacts only to specific triggers active at the moment, and responds with processing that gives off narratives in which transposable themes appear. While free-associating, these themes can then be lifted from the manifest context in which they emerge and placed into the original latent context that evoked them and to which they are an adaptive response. Genuine insight involves triggers and themes as they illuminate our indicators.

The analyzing/synthesizing phase of self-analysis is a challenge to our psychological and intellectual resources. In general, the hope at first should be modest: All you want is to understand something—anything—that has been trigger decoded and is new, no matter how small the gain. This quest for understanding involves an explanation— putting together themes with triggers in a way that brings fresh understanding to an issue or a symptom. There are three basic levels of insight:

Grade 1 insights are the ideal form of self-understanding. They connect specific and active trigger situations to specific themes derived from the narrative/associational complex; and they use this synthesized configuration to explain the unconscious side of an active indicator and propose a method for solution.

Archie is depressed. He dreams of Pearl Harbor. He recognizes themes of sneak attack, violence, death, and betrayal. He discovers a trigger: His job as an art director has been compromised by the hiring of a new artist. His unconscious perception—and unfortunately, it proved to be correct—is that the woman is being groomed to replace him. The trigger/theme complex explains the unconscious basis of his depression. The network can be decoded as an explanatory statement: Hiring that woman is part of a sneak attack through which I will be annihilated (lose my job); I am very depressed about that perception.

Archie's formulation and suspicions are confirmed by the unexpected recall of another dream fragment from the same night—a not uncommon type of validation. In the dream he is talking to Reggie, a former employee of his firm; Archie suddenly realizes that Reggie was replaced by a woman initially hired to be his assistant—the very fear/perception with which he himself is struggling.

Grade 2 insights also involve efforts at trigger decoding, but the results are incomplete. That is, you may identify a trigger situation that is at issue, but you're not able to integrate its implications with the available themes from the associational network in a way that generates a new piece of insight about an indicator. The triggers float without clear thematic ties. Still, you do come to understand something about the nature of your emotional issues at the moment; you also learn a bit about your sensitivities and vulnerabilities.

A second type of grade 2 insight involves themes without specifically defined triggers. Here a harvested yield from a narrative/associational network seems to bring no connection between the themes and active triggers. You know something about your unconscious stirrings—for example, that incestuous sexuality, or issues of loss, or of identity, are on your mind. But you know little of what has stirred up these issues. The themes float without triggers.

Tom knows that he's feeling stressed out by his car accident. He can't remember a dream so he invents a story about an accident, but it's too close to the real situation to encode unconscious meaning. His associations are either banal or related to other accidents and injuries.

Tom knows his trigger, but for the moment he has little in the way of encoded themes. Most important, he realizes his defensiveness and resistance to self-analysis and doesn't mistakenly think of his conscious thoughts as unconsciously derived insights. He also knows he must watch his feelings and behaviors for unconscious effects from the unmetabolized trigger episode and wait for another day when thematic threads will materialize.

Just the reverse happens to Sid, who has a nightmare about a storm at sea and being washed overboard from a schooner, then struggling to stay afloat. His associations go to a variety of incidents; some involve being caught in fires and other natural disasters, others touch upon striking sexual conflicts, while still others consist of disturbing acts of violence. Yet all Sid can find with respect to triggers are some minor irritations with his wife and one of his children, some tensions on his job where he's recently been promoted, and some minor conflicts with his friends.

Sid can be sure that images this frightening and powerful have been evoked by equally powerful triggers. All he can do is hold fast until he discovers what they are; for now at least he knows that something awful in terms of unconscious experience is afoot—it's a time to be watchful of his emotional responses and behavior and, through conscious vigilance, safeguard against self-harmful actions.

Grade 3 insights are a concatenation of so-called insights—widely accepted by psychotherapists and many laypeople—that are basically unsound and of little genuine help in solving emotional woes. Some may be benignly viewed as preliminary to trigger-decoded insight, others are basically false and self-deceptive.

You dream of death and propose that loss is on your mind; you dream of loss and realize that the death of your mother is connected to the recent death of your aunt. You recognize suddenly, not having been aware of it before, that you are angry, depressed, anxious, or acting badly. All such insights leave you open to major blind spots, active needs for self-deception and self-harm, pervasive defensiveness, limited knowledge, clever ways of avoiding critical trigger situations and unconscious meanings. They are preliminary at best, and harmful to your emotional health at worst. And no matter how seemingly perceptive and surprising these realizations may be, they will not help you solve problems and change behavior.

Insights come from analyzing and synthesizing. We've all got three piles to mix together to reach some conclusions: indicators, themes, and triggers. Indicators—depression, argumentativeness, obsessions—we mark as problems we want to explain in some depth. We put them in the back of our minds as difficulties whose unconscious (nonmanifest) meanings we are trying to grasp. In this way, we respect the fact that we, as humans, are target-oriented adaptive organisms and not generalizers—a problem is an exact problem and not an example of a class of problems, and a solution solves a precise problem and not a group of related issues.

So, with our target for insight established, we turn to our other two piles of information, determined to meld them together into a package of understanding. In one pile we have themes; in the other, triggers. The themes belong to a series of manifest stories—the origination narrative and the associations to that narrative. We proceed by taking a trigger situation, developing a sense of its evident implications, and then going to the collection of themes and placing each one together with the trigger experience. As we do this, we construct an explanatory sentence: This theme reflects how I have unconsciously experienced that trigger.

Initially we take the theme as a true and valid perception of a real but unconscious meaning of the trigger situation related to both ourselves and others. Only when the decoded meaning does not make common sense do we test out the theme as a possible directive as to how to deal with the trigger issues. We repeat this effort with all of the themes that we can identify, lifting them one by one out of the narrative/associational network and placing them beside the trigger at hand.

The collection of transposed themes is eventually shaped into a full statement of insight: I have experienced this trigger as this and that and the other, and my deep unconscious wisdom system is advising me to deal with it in this or that way (how interesting, because I hadn't realized any of this). Once we have united the themes with a particular trigger experience and decoded our unconscious wisdom, we move on to the next trigger and repeat the transposing process—though this time we include the previously analyzed trigger and our realized insights as part of the associational network that we will use in this fresh round of decoding.

We repeat the process until each known trigger has been connected to all known themes. While carrying out this analyzing/synthesizing process, new narratives may crop up. They should be allowed free play to be completed and subjected to associating and theme extraction. All new themes should be transposed into trigger situations already analyzed and with triggers yet to be explored. Fresh triggers also often come to mind along the way; naturally, these should be used as further receptacles for transposed themes drawn from the associational complex.

In this spiraling effort, glimpses of insight lead to fresh images, which in turn lead to still more insight. Retire from the effort only when the well runs dry. Though you can never be certain the job is fully done—and the opportunity for further work will always materialize—you're entitled to a sense of a job well done if you've put together even one synthesized fragment of fresh self-comprehension. Still, don't be surprised if something unexpected comes along before you put it all away; if that happens and time permits, simply take up where you left off and move mentally to where the new thoughts are taking you.

Leon's wife, Betsy, begins to complain that he is not working hard enough to cover the family's expenses. He responds with an elaborate self-defense, during which he includes a marginally related story that he'd read in the newspaper in which a man robbed a jewelry store and murdered the owner.

Without building an associative network yet, we can list the main themes in this out-of-context narrative. They include a newspaper story or something made public, a male robber, jewelry and store, murder, and a store-owner victim. Robbery and murder seem to be the most compelling themes. We now want to link these themes to the immediate trigger—Betsy's criticism of Leon's earning powers.

Leon consciously feels that there is some merit to Betsy's criticism; he hasn't been inclined to work overtime lately. But even so, he also feels that she is being quite unfair to him; he does try to earn enough money so the family will be in good shape financially. Besides, he muses, if she's so concerned about money, why doesn't she do more than free-lance an occasional book review for the Sunday paper?

To shift to the unconscious side of his experience, the themes of Leon's displaced story about an incident in the newspaper must be united with the trigger that evoked the narrative. We use the union to explain how Leon has unconsciously perceived his wife's criticism. Clearly the theme extraction and relocation process informs us—and Leon—that he feels attacked by his wife, somehow robbed of something valuable and destroyed.

This explanation makes common sense: Criticism is a kind of attack. And the imagery is also in keeping with the primitive qualities of unconscious experience and thinking. But we must not limit ourselves to Leon's unconscious perceptions of his wife; we must also formulate these themes as a reflection of his own unconscious stirrings and responses to the trigger situation. Leon himself harbors violence, and it is directed toward Betsy; unrecognized, these unconscious feelings and the needs that they evoke could wreak havoc in their marriage or could provoke either a symptom within or some kind of aberrant behavior by Leon. On the other hand, decoded and assimilated, these same unconscious reactions can be worked over and detoxified.

There is no evident indicator in the picture at the moment; but had Leon fought verbally—or even physically—with Betsy, the loss of control would have been based on his unconscious experience of her criticism and his unconscious response as well. The complex tie between triggers and themes are in essence the unconscious basis for emotional disturbance and self-defeating emotionally charged decisions.

In his quest for insight, Leon could have used this kind of self-analysis to understand that he had felt violently attacked by his wife and felt similarly inclined toward her. This insight was not available to his conscious system, where his reaction to the incident was milder and less infused with rage.

So far there is no unconscious validation of our formulation, nor any advice from Leon's deep unconscious system regarding how best to handle the situation. But all this was encoded in a brief association to the story Leon read in the newspaper: The wife of the dead man had revealed that their relationship had been far from peaceful. She seemed to feel guilty over his death, arguing that their combativeness had led him to be less than submissive to the thief; his bridling had led to his death. The wife had experienced a fresh distaste for hostility and violence. She had created a peace-without-violence committee that would raise funds to help underprivileged children, support family counseling, and help to rehabilitate known criminals. She believed deeply that every criminal could be redeemed if people knew how to reach out properly.

The first theme in this association is of a couple in conflict, who fought until disaster struck; this image confirms the sense of underlying violence between himself and Betsy that Leon had detected through decoding. Beyond that, the main themes are of forgiveness and reducing violence. Connecting these themes to the trigger of Betsy's criticism does not speak for direct perception—there was nothing conciliatory in her remarks. We therefore try next to formulate these themes, which in themselves sound like reparation and advice, as the solution to the tension proposed by Leon's encoded unconscious wisdom system. Make peace with your wife is the directive, offer her the olive branch that would signal the renunciation of your own vengeance as well.

Strangely enough, the associations also encoded a suggestion as to how Leon could earn more money. Leon was a stockbroker. About a year earlier, he had investigated a series of companies that manufactured and sold antiburglary devices. In the rush of other problems, he had never acted on the information he had collected, though he was aware of the earnings and progress of most of the companies. The unconscious message detectable in light of this particular trigger seemed to suggest that Leon should give serious thought to investing in that industry. Leon didn't simply take the advice of his encoded message at face value, but he did decide to take a closer look at the situation.

Anxiety operates many times over in the course of processing emotional experiences: It is anxiety that forbids the entry into awareness of many aspects of emotionally charged communications; anxiety that presses us to process much emotional meaning unconsciously; anxiety that prods us to encode the wisdom of the deep unconscious system; and anxiety that interferes with the trigger-decoding process itself, insisting that themes not be joined to the triggers to which they belong. But the human mind is resourceful and it can learn to master anxiety—and trigger decoding.

Cheryl is divorced and in her fifties, a high school history teacher. She has one child, Glenn, a man in his early twenties who suffers from anxiety attacks that interfere with his functioning. Through a bequest from his grandparents he's entered intensive psychotherapy and has taken to criticizing Cheryl harshly.

For her part, Cheryl has been grappling with feelings of guilt over her son's problem; she is also struggling in her relationship with Wally, the man whom she is currently dating. At times he seems quite aggressive, and Cheryl feels uncertain of their future together. Lately she has been feeling that she sees too much of Wally for their own good; they are both members of the social studies department in the private high school where Cheryl teaches.

The academic year is nearly over. One of her students, Brad, has invited his small social studies class to his house for a final farewell party—and Cheryl has agreed to the plan. Actually, she finds Brad a rather attractive teenager, mature beyond his years.

One morning Cheryl awakens holding on to a few fragments of a dream. She lies quietly in bed and more of the dream comes forth.

She is looking for Glenn, but he has disappeared; she can't find him anywhere. She's afraid he's been harmed or killed somehow. She tries calling him on the telephone—she's in an odd-looking phone booth—but gets Brad on the line instead. She's surprised to hear his voice, and even more surprised when Brad tells her he's in therapy with Glenn's analyst.

Given that the following day is the last day of class, and the day they will all go to Brad's house, Cheryl has little trouble fixing the dream in her mind for later self-analysis. (Linking a dream to a trigger—even an anticipated trigger—is a good way to increase the likelihood of keeping the dream with you for later processing.) But she also finds the dream disturbing, and wonders if it is a premonition of some kind—a thought she quickly dismisses, even though her sense of disquietude remains with her throughout the morning.

After an arduous day, Cheryl is finally in bed that night and able to take some time to turn inward and work with her dream. Though she has promised herself that she will free-associate to the dream, she is first drawn to its surface. She is aware of being worried about Glenn, that she sees him as a lost soul, and that at times she's fearful he's involved with illegal drugs and could do something terribly self-destructive with them. No surprises there, only Cheryl's realization that she is concerned about Glenn's continued distancing of himself and that she's worried about his safety. Cheryl has been able to pick up some of the contributions to her dream from her conscious system, and her current conscious worries have been clarified.

Cheryl's thoughts about Brad are a mixture of direct readings from the surface of her dream and the beginning of the associative process. She's surprised by the idea of his being in therapy with Glenn's therapist, but recalls that Brad has actually talked in class about his shrink, as he calls him, and how helpful the therapy has been; he was unable to talk in class when he began therapy, and he is quite comfortable doing so now.

Brad now brings some fresh and displaced (departure) images to mind. His mother is known around the school as a wild woman who will suddenly show up, barge into Brad's classroom, and begin talking to her son or to the teacher. Cheryl had gone through an incident of that kind, and it was difficult to handle the woman without enraging her or allowing her to disrupt the class. Cheryl had managed to ease her out of the classroom but dreaded a return visit. Brad had actually promised Cheryl that his mother wouldn't be there when they went to his house, but Cheryl had her doubts that his mother would stay away for the whole time.

Brad is an attractive young man, but Cheryl has noticed that even though he's known to have a girlfriend, he has wandering eyes and is often flirtatious not only with other female students but with the teachers as well. Brad is also physically chummy with several male students known to be homosexual; his seductiveness seems to be indiscriminate.

The telephone brings to Cheryl's mind a discussion at lunch two days earlier about obscene phone calls. One of the other female teachers had been receiving a number of such calls both directly and on her answering machine. It felt like an invasion of her privacy. The woman was taking countermeasures and changing and unlisting her telephone number, so the unwelcome caller would have no way of intruding into her space again. Beyond that, the telephone booth felt entrapping and reminds Cheryl of a time when Glenn as a very young boy had managed to get himself stuck in a phone booth and injured his finger in trying to extricate himself.

Cheryl pauses to collect her themes. She realizes that there is a lot here already; to keep associating would only make it more difficult to sort out the dream/associational network. The themes she finds most prominent are those of feeling cut off from others; concerns about death, entrapment, and injury; perverse invasions of one's privacy; allusions to psychotherapy—a curative process; and something about a mix-up of sorts through which two people whom she knows are both being seen by the same therapist.

In extracting themes from dreams and their associations, it is important to lift them from their immediate context into a more abstract space—to go from the specific to the general. We begin with concrete imagery related to particular people and places, lift out the general themes now divorced from those specific people and places, and keep them available to place into the trigger situations that will soon come to mind.

Armed with a bushel of themes, Cheryl now casts about for her triggers. She begins with the most obvious stimulus for this dream—the pending class meeting at Brad's house. Consciously Cheryl had thought of it as a nice gesture and felt that it would bring the school year to a close on a very pleasant note; Brad was said to live in a beautiful mansion. In fact, the idea hardly seemed to be an issue at all; why did it play such a prominent role in her dreams and associations?

To find the answer to this newly discovered indicator (and it's not uncommon to discover overlooked indicators in the course of self-analysis), Cheryl turns to her themes: being lost, noncommunication, death, entrapment, injury, seductiveness, invasion of privacy. She now tries to connect the themes to this trigger. Evidently, she says to herself, I unconsciously view my taking the class and myself to Brad's house as a way of getting lost, interfering with communication, a dangerous form of entrapment, injurious, and a sexualized invasion of his space. Some set of images, Cheryl observes. They are a complete surprise to her; what seemed like a nice gesture is unconsciously seen as a very dangerous and harmful, seductive intrusion.

Cheryl now thinks of her mixed reaction—one of excitement yet repudiation—to Brad's seductiveness, one of her other indicators. This seemed to characterize her unconscious view of his invitation—stimulating but inappropriate. Unexpectedly, Cheryl next thinks of a girl at school who has accused one of the male teachers of becoming physically seductive toward her. This encoded validating image seems to confirm the inappropriate and sexual qualities of this seemingly innocuous plan. Once more the conscious system and the unconscious system widely disagree.

Cheryl still tries to argue against the implications of her decoding efforts—the conscious system does not admit defeat willingly. But she begins to feel obliged to understand the basis for her encoded position and to not reject it because it runs so counter to her conscious assessment. It is disturbing to think that she's allowing Brad to seduce everyone in the class, including herself. She can only wonder about the unconscious effects that going to his home would have on her students.

It is becoming clear to Cheryl that she must reconsider the matter and find a way to rescind her acceptance of Brad's invitation. This advice from her deep wisdom system is encoded in the preventive measures taken by Cheryl's fellow teacher in order to block the male caller from invading her home. This set of themes also confirms Cheryl's unconscious perception that Brad's invitation is perverse and sexual (as are all such frame alterations— violations of the appropriate conditions of a relationship and its proper boundaries—no matter how much we consciously accept and justify these manipulations).

The theme of death, though it speaks of something deadly about this frame break, seems unfinished to Cheryl. When sources of anxiety appear in dream networks, they are best taken not only as perceptions of the unconscious meanings of a trigger situation but also as pointing to underlying factors that motivate the current emotional indicators. Where, then, might death anxiety be playing a role in Cheryl's life? By merely asking this question, the unpleasant but critical answer pops into her mind: About a year before Glenn had been conceived, Cheryl had lost a child soon after birth from a congenital heart defect, and this loss had occurred in late May. This was the anniversary of the incident, which unconsciously had much to do with many of Cheryl's current emotional problems.

The question now is how to extract these themes and place them as added unconscious perceptions of the trigger context of going to Brad's home. First, it would seem that Cheryl unconsciously saw the arrangement as destructive— a form of death that would disturb her and her students soon after the end of the semester—loosely, at the moment of birth. But in another sense, she is also unconsciously experiencing extending or breaking an established frame— that the class only meets in the classroom at school—as being the exception to laws and rules. The shift to Brad's house was a way of dealing with the end of the school year as a death-related experience—an ending. In light of this particular implication of the trigger situation—now formulated as the end of the academic year—the frame break was a way of saying: Look, death, the rule is that you follow life, but I'm going to show you that I can break rules and defy your rule as well. That is, going to Brad's house would unconsciously undo the effects of the final day of class and its reverberations by extending the boundaries of the classroom into the outside world—and if the classroom exists everywhere, then there is, in effect, no separation and loss when school ends. The images of being trapped in an enclosure and harmed seem to confirm this idea; they could well represent being in the womb and being injured—the creation of a congenital defect in utero.

We see again the unconscious validating process in action, confirming a formulation through fresh decoded realizations. When your decoded explanations lack this kind of support, reconsider what you have tentatively worked out. Often the key trigger has been missed. Looking for more associations to the prevailing origination narrative also aids the search for fresh ideas; these associations provide clues to both your missing triggers and your overlooked themes.

Cheryl decides to move on to the triggers. She takes her lead from her dream/associational network. Glenn is missing, perhaps dead—these themes continue to disturb her. Refusing to settle for her earlier general impressions, Cheryl now searches for a specific trigger to connect with these themes and with her son. Again to her surprise, a trigger occurs to her that she had thought about consciously but had not appreciated its power to disturb her.

Dr. Edwards, Glenn's therapist, had called Cheryl on the day before the dream to ask her to come to his office to discuss the young man's therapy. Cheryl made an appointment for the following week, but was consciously anxious about meeting the doctor; she was worried that he would hold her accountable for Glenn's problems. And she was also concerned that he would discover something terrible in her, tell her she's crazy—a fear she encoded in the allusion to Brad's mother.

The dream network echoes the feeling that the consultation would be entrapping and harmful; it is clearly both a moderate indicator and a strong unconscious concern. Cheryl's themes suggest unconscious perceptions and fantasies that the consultation will be the death of her; she will not want to or be able to communicate with Dr. Edwards. Their telephone conversation was enough; had she seen it unconsciously as intrusive and seductive as well?

Cheryl realizes that there are now more themes to connect with this trigger: The crazy mother comes up in another sense, as someone who intrudes inappropriately into her son's space. The perception here is that, in seeing Dr. Edwards, Cheryl is violating the privacy of her son's therapy; it would be as if she were in therapy with her son's therapist, intruding where she does not belong. In the dream, this encoded perception was most clearly represented in Brad being in therapy with Dr. Edwards and in the allusion to the obscene telephone caller. With a shudder, Cheryl takes note of the fact that her contact with Dr. Edwards had been by phone.

But there's still more that Cheryl can gather from her themes: While consciously she accepted the invitation to see Dr. Edwards and had only mild qualms about the visit, unconsciously her response was far more critical of the proposal. The interview is seen as a seduction, as perverse, and as a way of disrupting the communication between Glenn and Dr. Edwards; in the extreme, it is seen as the death—the end—of the therapy.

Cheryl has done more than simply lift her themes from their manifest context and transpose them into the trigger context. She has also cast about for themes that are interrelated and that help to shape a cogent series of logically related perceptions and meanings. In addition, she has derived some sage advice from her unconscious wisdom system: Reconsider the invitation, get your son's therapist out of your—or get yourself out of his—bedroom. Cheryl now must decide on her own how to handle this invitation in light of her unconscious insights into the matter.

To understand the unconscious part of life, we must continually integrate extracted themes with identified triggers. Self-analysis is enriching on many levels: It gives us a more incisive, nondeceptive picture of the present even as it illuminates the past. Only when the past becomes alive in the present can we resolve earlier issues. Every present-day trauma/trigger experience is an opportunity to develop more effective ways of dealing with our inner emotional issues and failures at coping. This effort is the road to a better future than might otherwise lie ahead for us.

11 ∘ Self-analysis with Others

ONE TOPIC REMAINS before we complete our efforts to master self-analysis: carrying out such work with one or more persons. While I have always thought of psychotherapy as a private endeavor, my experiences in teaching classes on decoding dreams and on self-analysis have led me to qualify this opinion.

There are three combinations to be considered: self-analysis with someone with whom you share an intimate relationship; with one or more persons with whom you have either a more distant connection or no prior relationship; and within the context of a class on the subject. Each of these settings is a mixed bag; each can enhance your pursuit of deep insight, and each can interfere.

Perhaps the most potentially treacherous context for self-analysis involves engaging in it with someone with whom you have a close relationship—husband or wife, close friend or lover, child or other relative. While I do believe that when this work is better understood, this kind of shared self-analysis will be in common use, I also suspect that under present conditions of relative unfamiliarity, this kind of intimacy is chancy. After all, we are dealing with encoded messages that have been disguised for good reason. Almost always, we have invoked this use of camouflage to protect not only ourselves as narrator but those whom we love. By violating this defensive maneuver, we can bring down much opprobrium from those around us—although it may have a constructive benefit. Under the guise of speaking to others candidly, we can use these unconscious messages and their decoded meanings as a form of hostility and attack, rather than as a loving form of insight.

All of us have a separate life lived out in the unconscious part of our minds. Some of it is more or less integrated into consciousness; much of it, however, remains unintegrated with our immediate experience and functioning. This underside of human experience is crude, primitive, intense, highly self-serving (though not without concerns for others); it is also frank, direct, nondefensive, and painfully outspoken. In the course of our everyday social lives, we take great pains to be far more even-tempered than we are in the deep unconscious system.

On the positive side, sharing self-analysis with someone close to you can open up channels of communication that would otherwise remain shut. This is especially true in situations of conflict where the driving forces are outside of the awareness of both parties.

Paul and Pam are both in their late twenties and live together. There's been a lot of tension between them lately, and both have talked about breaking up. Neither of them knows where the problem stems from; there's nothing obvious disturbing their relationship.

They decide to sit down together one night to see if they can figure out what the tension is all about. Paul is tired of Pam bugging him about his lack of concern for his appearance and his disinterest in keeping their apartment neat; he's also annoyed with her excessive frugality. On her side, Pam feels Paul is overstating things, and she adds a few complaints of her own. None of this is actually new; this is all recycled stuff. There must be something else going on, they conclude.

Pam suddenly remembers a fragment of a dream from the previous night:

> She is with her friend Ellie who is smiling joyfully.
> The setting is like a school or a hospital.

"Why Ellie?" Pam asks out loud. "Free-associate," advises Paul. "Ellie is my best friend," Pam starts, "you know that. I saw her the other day for lunch. She's looking real good. Of course—we went to school together, so maybe that's why the school is in there."

Recognizing that these associations are lacking in narrative elaboration, Paul presses Pam to find some specific incidents as associations to this dream. To himself, he has already connected the image of the hospital to Pam's abortion about a year ago, but he wisely decides not to introduce his own associations for now. A blunt association from the listener tends to distract rather than further the process. The offer of a sudden, out-of-the-blue interpretation is even more disruptive; early attempts at explanation long before there is a full dream/associational network tend to point the process toward intellectualizing and conscious system deliberations. Premature confrontations and queries about the details of a dream are similarly disruptive; they will generally mobilize the dreamer's defenses rather than enhance the flow of the material. Encouraging storied free associations to an origination narrative is the best the second party to a conjoint self-analysis can do.

Pam now recalls an incident when she and Ellie were in school. It concerns a time when Ellie missed her period and thought she was pregnant—only to discover that she was simply late. What could have triggered that set of themes? she wonders. (Meanwhile Paul takes this story as encoded confirmation of his own idea about the unconscious issue between himself and Pam; still, he correctly decides to bide his time before saying anything.) "Oh, of course, Ellie is pregnant now, isn't she? I guess I envy her a bit; she did mention that her doctor has his office at the hospital, so I guess that's where that image comes in. I don't know, I feel stuck again."

Paul presses her to associate further to the pregnancy and the hospital, and Pam suddenly remembers her abortion, a year ago in the hospital. She now recalls that she's been nauseous the past week and that Ellie's sister recently had twin girls. Her friend Mindy just broke up with the man she was living with because he wouldn't marry her and have children. Somehow, Pam now senses that these are her own underlying issues with Paul: She wants to get married and to have a child, but has said nothing about it because they had agreed to shelve these topics for at least another six months. Pam, whose career was moving forward very well, had thought she felt good about that decision; her dream/associational network clearly indicates that this is so only in her conscious feelings. Her unconscious position better accounts for her anger with Paul than do her conscious ideas.

Later, Pam associated the hospital with an attractive

doctor she had recently met through her job; Ellie had had an affair with her gynecologist at a time when her marriage was in trouble. Had Pam shared these associations with Paul, it probably would have been very difficult for him to accept Pam's confession of seductive designs on another man—even though such fantasies are an everyday occurrence on the unconscious level (when we have a problem with our lover, we unconsciously turn immediately to others to take his or her place; these unconscious reparative wishes are far different in structure from conscious desires to be unfaithful and from actions to that effect. One is unconscious and inevitable, and available for decoding before it leads to action, while the other is a conscious choice that carries with it a definite price tag). Confessions are a major risk in coupled processing.

If you decide to try self-analysis with a loved one, there are some principles to keep in mind. First, insure the confidentiality of what is said in these encounters. It is essential that what is shared during self-analysis—with whomever it might be—must not be recorded or reported on in any way. Without this assurance, there can be no sense of safety, no chance to play freely with images and triggers, and little likelihood of the kind of openness that is essential for meaningful self- and conjoint exploration.

Second, it seems best to stay away from mutual self-analysis when you are harboring secrets you really don't wish to share with the other person. Secrets should be handled through private processing so you can understand the unconscious basis of your behavior, its consequences for your current relationships, and the advice of your deep unconscious wisdom system on the matter. The decision as to whether to reveal a personal secret, to continue the behavior and the concealment, or to modify or eliminate the secretive behavior should be arrived at alone.

Engaging in self-analysis tends to arouse unresolved guilt and unconsciously to push people toward encoded—and sometimes direct—confessions. To do this without knowing you are doing it, and to do it through an encoded message that is sensitively picked up by the other person's deep wisdom system, is to open a can of worms that you think is tightly sealed. Conflicts are inescapable when one unconscious system speaks of painful matters to another unconscious system; this is a common unconscious basis for relationship tensions—and warfare.

Third, let the person who tells the dream or other origination narrative do most of the free-associating and engage in the initial search for triggers and themes. Let that person make the first attempts at analyzing and synthesizing; it's that person's narrative/associational network, and he or she has had the courage to express images with unconscious meanings—give the person a chance to discover the underlying messages first. Only his or her own associations will truly tap the personal symbolism involved. The listener should be a facilitator, encouraging free associations and the rest of the process without intruding his or her own ideas into the flow of the material—at least not for a while. He or she should detach a bit and become the observing party for the couple, the person who is watching for resistances, for clues to the mysteries—the indicators—you need to solve. In associating, a dreamer will often mention a story without giving it in detail; the facilitator can then serve their mutual self-analysis by asking for the story to be spelled out.

A listener's associations to someone else's dream usually confounds the self-analytic effort. They should be avoided except as a last resort—and then offered with great caution. And even more reserve is called for when a listener feels that he or she knows a veiled unconscious meaning that the other person seems to be overlooking. Resistances reflect both obstacles to self-analysis and much-needed protection.

Abrupt confrontative and unwarranted interpretative activity can cause much harm to the dreamer and to the relationship between the two parties to conjoint analyzing. There is much deserved resistance against trying to override a dreamer's defenses. The unwanted interpretation becomes an assault on the dreamer's conscious system; it is a way of misusing information and meaning that the other person is not prepared to handle and digest. The intruder's train of thought may also be off the mark and will derail the process. Even when the interpretation is correct in some substantial way, the dreamer will be unprepared mentally for its meaning and feel overwhelmed.

Fourth, if you decide to play hard ball, bring a good glove, abide by the rules, and expect the ball to sting your psyche. Know what you're getting into: that you're creating an open play space with another person within which some rather brutal messages will emerge if the processing works. Don't mope and feel bruised by what emerges; understand the language and mode of experience of the unconscious mind, and realize you're in a special relationship where a kind of truth is spoken that is quite unlike anything you have experienced consciously. Go into the experience with an open mind, determined to understand and resolve the issues whose deep meanings you wish to access; don't cry foul when it's fair play and what you asked for. Be tolerant and get the most you can from the frank insights that you reach together.

This touches on a fifth point: If you decide to engage in self-analysis with someone else, try to be certain that your motives are fundamentally constructive and reparative. This is not a process that wears well as a form of seduction, revenge, exhibitionism, or voyeurism; it has a way of turning against you if these are your motives. Conjoint self-analysis needs to be clean and well meaning; it reaches into too many thorny places to work unless both parties are sincere.

Related to this is a sixth point: Do some private self-analysis before joining in the process with another person. Be as clear as you can about your initial goals and your motives for involving the other person. Once underway, invoke your self-observing function to watch the process unfold. If a safe and secure frame cannot be established, or if the effort seems stalemated or hurtful, then think seriously of disbanding the processing partnership, at least for now. Monitor the process on all levels, and be alert for hurtful side effects. And pay attention to the emerging themes: One critical context—trigger—for the thematic material is most certainly the conjoint analyzing itself. If the themes are persistently negative and hurtful, and if compensatory positive imagery is lacking, there may well be something inappropriate about the partnership and/or how it is operating.

Seventh, keep in mind that you are not a psychotherapist and should not adopt such a role in conjoint work of this kind. You are trying to learn how to do self-analysis and to help the other person to learn and use the process as well—to find ways of overcoming obstacles to its effective use. You are not part of a psychotherapeutic couple, and there is no pledge from either party to say everything that comes to mind, as you would in formal therapy. The frame is educational rather than therapeutic, though it nonetheless requires total privacy (don't do this at a populated dinner table, or with anyone else within earshot). Also essential are complete confidentiality, mutual trust and forbearance, and a kind of humility and compassion that enables you to see that at bottom we all suffer from the same basic anxieties and the same sense of helplessness in the face of the ultimate hurts of life.

Eighth, joint self-analysis offers a particular advantage—one that accrues to all self-analysis in groups of two or more, though it also has certain risks as well. The most important triggers that give deep meaning to the conjointly constructed thematic network will stem from stimuli related to the setting and nature of the couple's relationship (in self-analysis classes, the teacher's actions and interventions are especially powerful triggers). Anyone with whom we engage in self-analysis becomes an overridingly important figure for the deep unconscious wisdom system, even if we consciously give that person little thought. And within that relationship, the framework or context within which the relationship has unfolded and its effects on the mutual self-analytic work are most critical.

The framework for any self-analysis group activity is one of the most important triggers for the participants' encoded wisdom systems and for the thematic networks they create. The closer your relationship with the person with whom you are doing this work, the more contaminated the unconscious experience and the more likely the generation of mixed images: both helpful and hurtful, incestuous and otherwise frame violating—and yet benignly curative. It is in understanding the threatening side of the conjoint processing experience that the most profound insights are usually discovered.

ooοο

We can extend these principles to all types of conjoint self-analysis. The emphasis in groups should be on learning how to carry out the process rather than on trying to cure someone else. In the course of the educational effort, some insights will be gained. But on the whole, these should come mainly in the privacy of each person's separate and individual efforts at self-understanding. The group functions best when it tries to demonstrate to a dreamer the nature of his or her obstacles to effective processing; in the course of such pursuits, each member of an analyzing group is likely to discover his or her own blind spots and resistances.

In trying to bring together a group of people determined to learn the art and skills of self-analysis, the more impersonal the outside relationship between the group members, the better the holding qualities and security of the group setting and the fewer the conflicts that are likely to be aroused. Ideally, the group should be constituted of people who are otherwise strangers to each other, though this is often difficult to arrange. Short of that, the next best arrangement is one that includes people who are not relatives and who are not close socially. The closer the ties between group members, the more intense the deep experience of seductive, aggressive, and rule-breaking elements. It is important to watch for these expressions and to properly understand their presence in light of the group's shared triggers. Failure to do this will often lead to what is called acting out—unconsciously sanctioned inappropriate behaviors including self-hurtful affairs, precipitous life changes, and such.

Classes should ideally be limited to about six people, and they should meet regularly, usually once weekly, for two hours—the amount of time needed for full processing and discussion. They should take place in a neutral and secluded place—perhaps a schoolroom or office where no class member works, and certainly not in someone's home.

People who engage in self-analysis learning groups tend to become so involved with the process that they are unable to step back and observe what has and has not been accomplished and/or missed—their self-vigilance is momentarily impaired. Because of this, I advise those who create such groups to select a leader who should keep that role for at least a month—it takes some time to get used to this position and to do it justice. The leader should not participate in the self-processing effort but should allow the group forty-five minutes for its exercise in analyzing, beginning always with a dream or some other origination narrative from a group member (who is the *designated narrator* for that session). While the group is trying to facilitate the narrator's attempts at self-analysis, the leader should remain the detached observer and forgo active involvement except to point out resistances that the group is having in engaging the narrator in the process. When the exercise is completed, he or she should lead the discussion. Being detached from the active processing enables the leader to point out where obstacles cropped up, when the group veered off from effective work, where it missed critical triggers and themes.

If you are fortunate enough to find a professional therapist capable of leading this kind of self-analysis group in which trigger decoding is the essential tool, he or she takes the role of permanent leader. The therapist does not engage in the self-analysis exercise, maintains the frame of the group experience, and avoids self-revelations and frame breaks of his or her own. Most important, he or she must be capable of consistent vigilance over the process at hand

and of identifying group-related triggers; this is often difficult, because the triggers generally involve the leader and any and all of the frame alterations and inadvertently revealed vulnerabilities that he or she has been involved in. The resultant encoded images are distinctly unflattering to the group leader, who must resist his or her own natural tendencies to avoid such realizations. While these triggers also tend to disturb group members, they lend themselves admirably for learning self-analysis.

Just as learning occurs in psychotherapy, there appears to be some therapeutic benefit in the course of learning self-analysis, but this gain is coincidental rather than primary. While some therapists are likely to try these principles of self-analysis in a therapeutic group, I have not been so inclined. In my experience, groups are for education, while private dyads are for psychotherapy. It is the educational frame that seems to facilitate the learning process and make this type of experience work well. Shading the work toward therapy clouds the situation and modifies the frame in ways that disturb more than enhance. This does not preclude the leader's use of illustrative interpretations when the thematic/trigger material facilitates such interventions; it merely stresses the limited nature of such interventions and their educational rather than therapeutic intentions.

This brings us to the differences between formal psychotherapy and self-analysis classes. In the former, the goal is distinctly therapeutic and the frame is strictly defined, as are the respective roles of patient and therapist. The patient is pledged to free-associate without restriction, and the therapist is committed to sound interactional interpretations based on the appropriate use of trigger decoding. When symptom relief occurs, therapy is terminated.

Self-analysis classes are designed to teach the process as

a learning experience rather than a therapeutic endeavor. There is a clear frame, but departures from the ideal are better tolerated than in therapy as long as they are within reasonable limits—for example, a chance meeting with the leader outside of the class, or a brief and impersonal self-revelation on his or her part; such incidents are workable in these classes yet could be quite disturbing in therapy. On the other hand, a social contact between the leader and a group member or personal revelations by the leader are likely to be very disruptive to the learning process—as they are in a therapy experience. All efforts to enter the domain of unconscious expression create extreme sensitivity to the role definitions, setting, and other conditions of the pursuit—the encoded wisdom system is highly sensitive to the circumstances under which its secrets are revealed.

In general, a leader will occasionally offer a model decoded interpretation based on material developed in a self-analysis exercise. Most of the leader's comments are explanatory and educational; they may include teaching about the structure of the mind, the nature of conflict and emotional disturbance, the details of the theory behind self-analysis itself, the techniques of the process, and any other relevant topic that emerges from class exercises.

Learning self-analysis is grounded in living dreams and trigger issues primarily because it is impossible to learn the process any other way. Nonetheless, the students or group members are *not* committed to tell all; conscious concealment is accepted and unconscious guardedness expected. The student stops attending these classes when he or she feels that the process has been sufficiently mastered to proceed on his or her own, not at a moment of cure.

Clearly, each situation—therapy and self-analysis classes—offers something distinctive. In the main you obtain a cure through effective therapy (and you may, but often don't, learn the process), while the classes give you the process (through which you may effect your own cure). People turn to therapy only when they are undergoing unbearable emotional suffering; people use classes when they want to reduce such suffering on their own and also want to have a better grasp of the influence of unconscious experience on their lives. Each supplements the other. Together they may well be the ultimate healing experience.

12 ◦ The Results of Self-analysis

THE GOALS OF self-analysis are multilayered. The bottom line is the best possible emotional life a person can have over the short and long terms. Intermediate goals are accessing and using our own deeply unconscious wisdom; gaining trigger-decoded insights; aiding the hapless conscious system in managing our emotional affairs; teaching the conscious system new ways of coping; providing the conscious mind with information and meaning it can use but prefers to avoid; modifying the costly defenses of the conscious system; weakening the devastating but natural alliance between the unconscious fear/guilt system and the conscious system; enlarging our capacity for self-observation and for emotional adaptation; and, to paraphrase an early proposition of Freud's, making all sides of unconscious experience conscious for examination—both the fears and the knowledge.

Each point has consequences for the realities of your life and the expansion of your awareness of yourself and the world about you. More than offering solutions to pressing emotional concerns, self-analysis enables us to develop fundamental coping skills that will make life easier no matter what comes up. By doing effective self-analysis and arriving at fresh and meaningful decoded insight, just about all of these goals can be reached.

Among the aims of self-analysis, those that pertain to modifying our direct ways of coping are especially important. The conscious system is set in its ways and has limited vision when it comes to its own flaws, costly errors, poor choices, dysfunctional behavior patterns, lack of insight, and the degree to which its choices are unconsciously driven. In this context, we can state a goal of self-analysis as compelling and coercing the conscious system to change both its views and its ways of coping.

The final results of trigger decoding should be startling. How are you to know beforehand about a life you've never led, a kind of decision you've never made before, a solution you never thought of, a way of relating you've never experienced? The positive results of trigger decoding are not confined to gradual change. In an acute emotional emergency and at times of a major life decision, you have no better resource than the encoded wisdom system and its brilliant and incisive points of view. An ounce of encoded insight is worth a ton of conscious deliberations.

Perhaps the most fitting way to end this book is with one last vignette, an incident that was told to me just the other day. It came from my friend George, whose daughter, Nell, recently got engaged to be married. At the engagement party, George was offering his daughter congratulations and best wishes but found himself blocked. Consciously he had somehow found himself opposed to the match from the outset; there was something about Lloyd, Nell's fiancé, that he didn't trust, but he hadn't said anything to his daughter regarding his doubts about the liaison.

Embarrassed by his loss of words, he turned crimson. But his daughter sensed his difficulty and took his hand and gently advised him, "Why not just say what Churchill said: 'Courage!' 'Courage indeed,' " was his rejoinder. He paused, but then went on: "Churchill—wasn't he the man who told the story of being at a formal dinner, seated next to a woman who found his eating habits crude? Yes, I think it was he," George reflected, warming up to his story. "So the woman turned to Churchill and said, If I were your wife, I'd feed you poison. And if I were your husband, Churchill came back at her, I'd take it!"

You'll probably never find a more concise and easily decoded out-of-context story, though only the first level of meaning is transparent; for the rest we'd need George's free associations. But for the moment, his overriding unconscious perception of his daughter's pending marriage is virtually self-decodable—it's a way of taking poison, of being murdered. Later, with this incisive image haunting him, George was able to justify his encoded perception by recalling several stories of violence Lloyd had recounted that formed the basis for George's concern that he would someday harm his daughter.

But there was another side to this equation. George was projecting onto his daughter and future son-in-law his unconscious perceptions of his own marriage, which was in some difficulty at the time—George's own indicator and trigger for this image. Still deeper was the guilt and anxiety that George was experiencing for an affair he was having—something he had already confided to me. While consciously George saw the involvement as playful and innocuous, he could see now that his unconscious view was rather different: It was an act of murder toward his wife, and probably his mistress as well, and a poisonous deed that called for the retaliatory punishment of death to George himself—a realization that helped to explain a recent car accident for which he was largely responsible.

George had been very close to openly opposing Nell's pending marriage and also to separating from his wife. By associating to the story element of poison, he recovered a series of memories related to an overdose of pills his mother had taken in a suicide gesture when George was a child; other associations enabled him to clarify a number of issues within his marriage related to his wife's rather strong objections to his self-indulgences of food and liquor—George was obese and might well have been using food to poison himself to death.

These insights into his unconscious view of marriage enabled George to modify his reaction to Lloyd—it was far more favorable on balance than George had realized—and to look more approvingly on the engagement, thereby avoiding a rupture in his relationship with his daughter. And he was now in a position to continue to analyze the issues between himself and his wife. In fact, he was planning to give up the affair and initiate efforts to get closer to his wife. And even though all I did was listen silently to his self-conscious story, George thanked me for turning him on to self-analysis—it helped him to get things straight.

Ultimately, the most meaningful self-analysis must be done in the privacy of your own chambers and solely with your own thoughts. Everything else is secondary and geared to support your own personal efforts. On that score, remember that this is a process slowly learned, filled with small skirmishes from which you can discover a great deal whether you win or lose for the moment. Self-analysis is a technique that is never settled and easy, but it is never without the capacity to give you truly fresh insights into yourself. Few efforts in life can give you more.

Index